New Frontiers in Guadalupan Studies

New Frontiers in Guadalupan Studies

EDITED BY
VIRGILIO ELIZONDO
AND
TIMOTHY MATOVINA

◥PICKWICK *Publications* • Eugene, Oregon

NEW FRONTIERS IN GUADALUPAN STUDIES

Copyright © 2014 Wipf and Stock Publishers. All rights reserved. Except for brief quotations in critical publications or reviews, no part of this book may be reproduced in any manner without prior written permission from the publisher. Write: Permissions, Wipf and Stock Publishers, 199 W. 8th Ave., Suite 3, Eugene, OR 97401.

Pickwick Publications
An Imprint of Wipf and Stock Publishers
199 W. 8th Ave., Suite 3
Eugene, OR 97401

www.wipfandstock.com

ISBN 13: 978-1-62564-208-0

Cataloging-in-Publication data:

New frontiers in guadalupan studies / edited by Virgilio Elizondo and Timothy Matovina.

p. ; cm. —Includes bibliographical references and index.

ISBN 13: 978-1-62564-208-0

1. Guadalupe, Our Lady of. I. Elizondo, Virgilio P. II. Matovina, Timothy M., 1955–. III. Title.

BT660.G8 N49 2014

Manufactured in the U.S.A.   09/15/2014

Excerpts from Bernardino de Sahagún's Florentine Codex: General History of the Things of New Spain courtesy of The University of Utah.

Image credits:

Figure I: La Virgen de Guadalupe, Juan de Correa. Museo Nacional de Escultura, Valladolid, Spain. Ministerio de Educación, Cultura y Deporte (CE1679).

Figure II: Indulgence for alms toward the erection of a church dedicated to the Virgin of Guadalupe, Samuel Stradanus. The Metropolitan Museum of Art, Gift of H. H. Behrens, 1948 (48.70).

Figure III: Stradanus detail. The Metropolitan Museum of Art, Gift of H. H. Behrens, 1948 (48.70).

Contents

Images | *vi*
Preface | *vii*
 —Virgilio Elizondo and Timothy Matovina
Acknowledgments | *xi*

1 Our Lady of Guadalupe in Bernardino de Sahagún's
   Historia general de las cosas de Nueva España | 1
   —Yongho Francis Lee

2 "May You Be Joyful, Oh Saint Mary" | 19
   Translating and Transforming Marian Devotion in New Spain
   —Katharine Mahon

3 Our Lady of Guadalupe in Art, 1606–1688: Growing the Devotion | 39
   —Kate Macan

4 The Huei tlamahuiçoltica | 65
   Responding to Pastoral Challenges in Light
   of Our Lady of Guadalupe
   —Alison Fitchett Climenhaga

5 Mother of Health, Remedy for the Plague | 88
   Preaching on Guadalupe in the Midst of Death
   —Michael Griffin

6 The Guadalupan Covenant | 108
   An Evaluation of the Nican mopohua *in*
   Light of the Ancient Jewish Tradition
   —Colleen Cross

7 Apocalypse at Tepeyac | 125
   —Michael Anthony Abril

Index | 155

Images

Figure I: *Virgen de Guadalupe*, Juan de Correa. Museo Nacional de Escultura, Valladolid, Spain. Ministerio de Educación, Cultura y Deporte (CE1679). | 60

Figure II: *Indulgence for alms toward the erection of a church dedicated to the Virgin of Guadalupe*, Samuel Stradanus. The Metropolitan Museum of Art, Gift of H. H. Behrens, 1948 (48.70). | 61

Figure III: Stradanus detail. The Metropolitan Museum of Art, Gift of H. H. Behrens, 1948 (48.70). | 62

Preface

DEVOTION TO OUR LADY of Guadalupe has evolved for nearly five centuries into a deeply rooted, multifaceted tradition. Guadalupan studies, however, have tended to focus on the origins of her cult rather than its evolution. The inordinate attention given to this debated topic overshadows scholarly attention to an equally vital question: Given the plentiful miraculous images of Christ, Mary, and the saints that dotted the landscape of colonial Mexico, how did the Guadalupe cult rise above all others and emerge from a local devotion to become a regional, national, and then international phenomenon? Extant documentation suggests that for its first two centuries Guadalupan devotion spread gradually. Guadalupe paintings, medals, sermons, *cofradías* (confraternities or pious societies), and feast day celebrations increased incrementally, as did the choice of Guadalupe as a name for places, children, shrines, and churches. Initially concentrated in Mexico City and the environs, it was not until the time of Mexican independence in 1821 that the veneration of Guadalupe permeated the territories of the newly formed nation. A number of factors contributed to Guadalupe's rising acclaim, most notably her devotees' multitudinous testimonies about her compassion and miraculous aid, the foundational influence of the earliest theological writings on Guadalupe, the urban networks that linked other municipalities to the trend-setting center of Mexico City, her multivocal appeal to diverse castes and races, and her role in the rise of Mexican national consciousness.

Essays in this volume enhance the growing body of literature that traces the development of the Guadalupe tradition, examining a range of topics that span the Guadalupe cult's sixteenth-century origins to the milestone of Pope Benedict XIV establishing an official liturgical feast for Guadalupe in 1754. Yongho Francis Lee provides an astute reexamination of Bernardino de Sahagún's treatment of Guadalupe in his monumental *Historia general de las cosas de Nueva España* (ca. 1576), especially the often-cited passage in which Sahagún accuses natives of continuing to worship the pre-Columbian mother of the gods Tonantzin under the guise of venerating Guadalupe. Katharine Mahon also examines early missioners

preface

like Sahagún. She assesses the understanding of Mary presented to the natives in sermons, prayer texts, and devotions, illuminating the importance of studying the Guadalupe tradition within the wider context of the promotion and reception of Marian piety in the New World.

Two essays investigate the ongoing evolution of the devotion in the seventeenth century. Focusing on the inculturation theme and a primary source Mahon also highlights, Alison Fitchett Climenhaga evaluates the evangelization strategy in the first Guadalupan pastoral manual, Luis Laso de la Vega's *Huei tlamahuiçoltica* (1649). She illuminates both the pastoral response the manual recommends for apostolic work among seventeenth-century Nahuas, as well as its implications for contemporary inquiry into the theology of mission. Given that most devotees knew about Guadalupe not from written texts but from art and oral tradition, Kate Macan maps the relationship between artistic representations of Guadalupe and the spread of the devotion. She dates her study strategically from the first known reproduction of the Guadalupe image in 1606 to the exaggerated 1688 claim of Guadalupe enthusiast Francisco de Florencia that every church in Mexico had an altar dedicated to her.

Michael Griffin's essay probes the catalytic event for the official declaration of Guadalupe as patroness of New Spain, the disastrous *matlazahuatl* (typhus or typhoid fever) epidemic of 1736–1737, which claimed more than forty thousand lives in Mexico City alone. City residents attributed the abatement of the epidemic to Guadalupe's intercession, publicly acclaimed her as their patroness, and incited leaders in other towns and municipalities to do the same. This chain of events culminated in 1754 when Pope Benedict XIV declared Guadalupe the patroness of New Spain and named December 12 her feast day. Griffin analyzes the pivotal sermon that Father Bartolomé Felipe de Ita y Parra offered at the Guadalupe shrine during the epidemic, and examines the implications of Ita y Parra's oration for communal responses to plague, particularly as articulated in the writings of René Girard.

Theological writings about Guadalupe spanning more than three and a half centuries have long shaped and been shaped by the contours of Guadalupan devotion. Strikingly, from the first published theological work on Guadalupe, Miguel Sánchez's 1648 book *Imagen de la Virgen María*, down to the present, those who have explored the theological meaning of Guadalupe have not focused primarily on typical Marian topics, such as her title *Theotokos* ("God bearer" or Mother of God), perpetual virginity,

preface

Immaculate Conception, and Assumption. Rather, theologians have examined the Guadalupe image, apparitions account, and its historical context as a means to explore the collision of civilizations between the Old and the New Worlds and the ongoing implications of this clash for Christianity in the Americas and beyond. Today Guadalupe is most frequently associated with both the struggle to overcome the negative effects of the conquest of the Americas and the hope for a new future of greater justice, faith, and evangelization. Theologies of Guadalupe are thus an ongoing effort to articulate a Christian response to one of the most momentous events of Christianity's second millennium: the conquest, evangelization, and struggles for life, dignity, and self-determination of the peoples of the Americas.

While all the essays in this volume encompass theological analyses, two of them contribute most directly to the ongoing development of theological works on Guadalupe. Colleen Cross considers the notion of covenant in the Guadalupe tradition, particularly as evidenced in the text of the *Nican mopohua* (a title derived from the document's first words, "here is recounted"), the Nahuatl-language apparitions account that devotees esteem as the foundational text of that tradition. Cross compares the Guadalupan notion of covenant to its meaning in Judaism and Christianity, furthering the understanding of this pivotal concept of biblical faith. Similarly, Michael Anthony Abril deepens understanding of a particular theological theme through comparative analysis, in his case the theme of apocalyptic. He explicates the importance of apocalyptic in Guadalupan theological writings from Miguel Sánchez down to the present day. Then he engages in a mutually enriching dialogue between these writings and contemporary apocalyptic thought, particularly in the works of René Girard and Johann Baptist Metz.

The University of Notre Dame's Institute for Latino Studies provided funding for copyright fees and editorial assistance for this volume. We are also grateful to Mary Reardon, who did superb work as copy editor for the manuscript. We also acknowledge the University of Utah Press for permission to cite the English translation of Bernardino de Sahagún's *Historia general de las cosas de Nueva España*.

The genesis of this volume is a doctoral seminar called Guadalupe: Faith, Theology, and Tradition that we team teach at the University of Notre Dame. To our knowledge, this is the only doctoral seminar dedicated entirely to Guadalupan studies. Students from this course are the authors in this volume. They represent various theological areas of study in our

preface

department: Liturgical Studies, Moral Theology, Systematic Theology, and World Religion, World Church. We are honored to have been part of the theological formation of these talented and dedicated young scholars. This publication of their work is in the Latin American tradition of a *cuaderno* (literally "notebook"), a first presentation of new research that shows great promise for further developing a field of study. Collectively their essays make a substantial contribution to theologies of Guadalupe and to scholarly investigations of how early Guadalupan devotion grew from its local origins to national prominence. Our hope is that, like us, you as reader will learn much from their insightful research.

Virgilio Elizondo and Timothy Matovina
University of Notre Dame

Acknowledgments

Virgilio Elizondo is the Notre Dame Professor of Pastoral and Hispanic Theology and is widely acclaimed as "the father of U.S. Latino religious thought." His numerous honors and accomplishments include the founding of the influential Mexican American Cultural Center in 1972, his transformative leadership and establishment of the internationally televised *Misa de las Americas* when he served as rector at San Fernando Cathedral in San Antonio from 1983 to 1995, and his recognition as one of *Time* magazine's spiritual innovators for the new millennium.

Timothy Matovina is Professor of Theology and Executive Director of the Institute for Latino Studies at the University of Notre Dame. He has authored or edited fifteen books, most recently *Latino Catholicism: Transformation in America's Largest Church* (2012). Matovina and Elizondo have also collaborated on various previous publications, including *San Fernando Cathedral: Soul of the City* (1998) and *The Treasure of Guadalupe* (2006).

The seven authors of this volume were students in a doctoral seminar called "Guadalupe: Faith, Theology, and Tradition" that the editors team teach at the University of Notre Dame.

1

Our Lady of Guadalupe in Bernardino de Sahagún's *Historia general de las cosas de Nueva España*

Yongho Francis Lee

FRAY BERNARDINO DE SAHAGÚN (ca. 1499–1590), a Franciscan missionary to sixteenth-century New Spain, left one of the most meaningful accounts of religious practices at Tepeyac in the sixteenth century in his *Historia general de las cosas de Nueva España* (*General History of the Things of New Spain*, often commonly referred to as the *Florentine Codex*).¹ The encyclopedic *General History* was originally written in Nahuatl, the native language of the Nahuas, with the help of native assistants, in 1559 through 1569. A systematic production of a Spanish version dating to the mid-1570s followed. A bilingual version with Nahuatl and Spanish was compiled twice, during the years 1567–1577 and 1578–1579.²

Sahagún's rare mentions of the shrine and devotion at Tepeyac in the *General History* are from two notes of the Spanish version of the work's *Book XI*, which does not have corresponding Nahuatl translations. These accounts have been examined in two kinds of discourse primarily: either in a debate of the authenticity and historicity of Mary's apparition and

---

1. Poole, *Our Lady of Guadalupe*, 69–81.

2. The second bilingual version of the *General History* is preserved and known as the *Florentine Codex*, as it is kept in the Biblioteca Medicea Laurenziana in Florence. For details on the production history of the *General History*, see Anderson and Dibble's introductions to Sahagún, *Introductions and Indices*.

manifestation of the image on the *tilma* of Juan Diego in 1531,[3] or in investigations of the syncretistic characteristic of the Mexican religious practices in the post-conquest period.[4]

Many scholars have mined Sahagún's twelve books of the *General History* to deepen their understanding of the religion, culture, society, and natural environment of New Spain before and after the Spanish conquest. Overall, the data offered by Sahagún is abundant in its volume, diverse in its contents, and scientific in the methodology used to collect it, as Sahagún is considered as the first "ethnographer" of America. Sahagún's relatively brief references concerning Our Lady of Guadalupe provided scholars—through many centuries—with direct information and clues to help reconstruct a religious phenomenon that reportedly occurred in the early stages of the conquest. His original and primary purpose with the *General History*, however, was not ethnographic or scientific, but to have the work serve as a tool in his and other missionaries' task of converting the Nahuas. It is necessary to read his Guadalupe texts with this perspective in mind.

When it comes to Guadalupe, it is clear that Sahagún was most concerned with the danger of syncretistic religious practices disguising ancient paganism as the newly emerging Marian devotion among the Nahua people. However, a warning to readers of such suspicious devotional practice is not all that can be drawn from the record of this affair. Sentiments of despair, affection, and hope are embedded in the written account of Guadalupe. There is also more that can be read between the lines.

To start off with, this paper will examine Sahagún's explicit missionary intention in compiling the *General History* in light of the early Franciscan mission in New Spain. Then this essay will chronicle his general understanding of and ambivalent attitude toward Nahua culture, religion, and society. Lastly, with these items in mind, this essay will closely analyze Sahagún's texts concerning the religious practices in Tepeyac and at other Christian shrines. The primary sources for this investigation are Sahagún's prologues and appendices to the twelve books of the *General History*, where the accounts of Guadalupe are found.

---

3. Poole, *Our Lady of Guadalupe*, 77–81, and Brading, *Mexican Phoenix*, 214–15.
4. Kroger and Granziera, *Aztec Goddesses*, 143.

BERNARDINO DE SAHAGÚN AND HIS INTENTION WITH GENERAL HISTORY OF THE THINGS OF NEW SPAIN

Bernardino de Sahagún was born in 1499 in Sahagún, in the region of Tierra de Campos, Spain. He joined the Order of the Friars Minor (Franciscan) while he was still studying at the University of Salamanca. The combination of Franciscan formation and education in Salamanca affected the young Franciscan, as manifested in his life and writings. At that time, like other European universities, Salamanca was immersed in the Renaissance.[5] One of the important academic trends, which heavily influenced Franciscan intellectuals including Sahagún, was the emphasis on the Sacred Scriptures for a renewal of Christian life. This focus naturally increased the interest in linguistics and in a proper interpretation and translation of the Bible to benefit other Christians. In light of these trends, Franciscan missionaries made formidable efforts to learn indigenous languages in order to teach the Gospel in the native languages of the Nahuas since their first landing in the New World.[6]

Franciscan millenarianism also greatly motivated their evangelical zeal. The Franciscans, in particular Observant friars, who insisted on returning to the life of simplicity and poverty lived by St. Francis of Assisi, envisioned the establishment of the primitive church or the Indian church in New Spain, modeled after the church of the Apostolic era. This new church should be free from the falsehood, superstitions, and any sort of corruption that were prevalent in Europe. Influenced and shaped by these intellectual and spiritual trends, twelve Franciscans arrived in New Spain in 1524, followed by many other Franciscans, including the young Franciscan Bernardino de Sahagún, who reached the new land in 1529. His *General History* should be read against this background.

General History of the Things of New Spain is a monumental encyclopedia of the Nahua world. A significant amount of valuable content in the work and his own development of research methodology[7] are more than

---

5. At this university, Sahagún might have studied various subjects such as languages, canon law, moral theology, theology, mathematics, music, medicine, and arts. As León-Portilla suggests, those studies must have helped him in his missionary life in New Spain and in his composition of the *General History*. León-Portilla, *Sahagún: First Anthropologist*, 38–39.

6. Ibid., 26–70.

7. Sahagún describes the process of research, compilation, and translation of the work in the prologue to *Book II*.

enough to entitle him to be understood as the "first anthropologist" in the modern sense.[8]

However, Sahagún, like all the Franciscan missionaries, dedicated his life to the divine task of evangelization of the Nahua people, and his linguistic, ethnographic interest and achievements were to serve to that end. Miguel León-Portilla comprehensively evaluates Sahagún's works in this light, saying, "Only by knowing their language, their mentality, and their way of life would it be possible to bring them the message of Christianity in their own cultural context, as was the main object of the friars' activities."[9]

The early Franciscan missionaries were elated with the seemingly successful result of their zealous missionary work, seeing many of the recently conquered Nahuas converting and becoming Christians. However, before long they were dismayed and perplexed at the reality that the neophytes had not totally abandoned their ancient pagan beliefs and were still practicing their ancient religion outside of the surveillance of the missionaries. Pagan songs were of particular concern. Although pagan rituals could be easily identified, pagan songs were hard to recognize unless the listener knew the language, and Sahagún was concerned that outside the awareness of the missionaries, pagan songs were being sung openly, "without its being understood what they are about, other than by those who are natives and versed in this language, so that, certainly, all he desires is sung, be it of war or peace, or praises to himself, or of scorn of Jesus Christ, without being understood by the others."[10]

In some places, even the worship of ancient pagan gods and goddesses continued under the guise of Christian celebration of saints without the missionaries' awareness of this fact. Sahagún insists, "I verily believe that there are many other places in these Indies where reverence and offerings to the idols are clandestinely practiced under the pretext of the feasts which the Church celebrates to revere God and His saints" (Note Also, originally

---

8. León-Portilla, *Sahagún: First Anthropologist*, 24. Anderson and Dibble attribute Sahagún's anthropological masterpiece in part to his education, heavily influenced by the humanist Renaissance movement. See Anderson and Dibble's introductions to Sahagún, *Introductions and Indices*, 35. For the education of Sahagún and the influence of Renaissance, see León-Portilla, *Sahagún: First Anthropologist*, 26–70.

9. León-Portilla, "Significado de la obra de Fray Bernardino de Sahagún," 21. Quoted in Anderson and Dibble's introductions to Sahagún, *Introductions and Indices*, 34.

10. Sahagún, *Introductions and Indices*, prologue to Book II, 58.

from *Book XI*, but sourced in this essay from *Introductions and Indices*, 92–93).[11]

Sahagún, who was fluent in Nahuatl and well acquainted with Nahua religion, culture, and customs, was certain that "The sins of idolatry, idolatrous rituals, idolatrous superstitions, auguries, abuses, and idolatrous ceremonies are not yet completely lost" (prologue to *Book I*, 45). Primarily concerned by this reality, Sahagún intended to compose the *General History* in order to help Christian missionaries recognize the still-active idolatrous practices and lead the pagan people and not-yet fully Christianized neophytes to the true Christian faith.

For Sahagún, this re-evangelizing process was comparable to the task of an adept medical doctor: "The preacher and confessors are physicians of the souls for the curing of spiritual ailments" (prologue to *Book I*, 45). In the prologue to the first book of the *General History* entitled "The Gods," setting out to enumerate and describe the ancient Nahua pantheon, Sahagún compares the acquisition of diverse knowledge of the Nahua religion to a medical survey required to correctly diagnose the disease of a patient, to find the origin of the disease, and to administer a proper cure for the ailment. In the case of the Nahua people, the disease is not a physical one but a spiritual one, and the cure of the ailment is entrusted to the spiritual physician or the preacher and the confessor.

In a medical procedure, it is necessary to efficiently communicate with a patient in order to know the exact symptoms and to identify the disease from which the patient suffers. Likewise, preachers and confessors should be capable of communicating with the Nahuas to detect their spiritual ailments. Sahagún seems frustrated at the reality that idolatrous practices are sometimes conducted in the presence of missionaries without their awareness, not only because of their lack of knowledge of the ancient idolatry but also because of their incompetence in Nahuatl.

> To preach against these matters, and even to know if they exist, it is needful to know how they practiced them in the times of their idolatry, for, through [our] lack of knowledge of this, they perform many idolatrous things in our presence without our understanding it. . . . And the confessors neither ask about them, nor think

11. See also the following comment: "After their conversion here, they sing some songs they have composed, which deal with the things of God and His saints, they are surrounded by many errors and heresies. And even in the dances and celebrations many of their ancient superstitions and idolatrous rituals are practiced, especially where no one resides who understands them." Sahagún, prologue to *Book X*, 83.

that such a thing exists, nor understand the language to inquire about it, nor would even understand them, even though they told them of it.¹²

As Sahagún stresses the need of language proficiency, he clearly gave thought to facilitating linguistic training for missionaries when he compiled the *General History*: "This work is like a dragnet to bring to light all the words of this language with their exact and metaphorical meanings, and all their ways of speaking, and most of their ancient practices, the good and evil" (prologue to *Book I*, 47). Sahagún assures readers that the *General History* will help those who intend to learn Nahuatl achieve their goal "with much less effort than it costs [him]" in his work on the *General History*, which had required laborious research and a protracted compiling process from him and his native assistants (prologue to *Book I*, 47).¹³

Besides the knowledge of Nahua religion, language, and customs, Sahagún argues that even the knowledge of material things, which the *General History* discusses in great amount, would ultimately be a good aid in undertaking the task of evangelization more effectively and accurately. In the prologue to *Book XI: Earthly Things*, he insists that making an appropriate reference to familiar customs and material things is a very effective way to deliver the message of the Gospel. He bases his argument on the exemplar of Jesus: "In order to give examples and make comparisons, in the preaching of the gospel, a knowledge of the things of nature is certainly not the least noble jewel in the coffer. We see the Redeemer as having used it" (prologue to *Book XI*, 87). Sahagún also expected that he would facilitate the Nahuas in disassociating created things from divinity by informing them of the scientific knowledge about material things.

Thus, first motivated by his assurance of the need for knowledge of the indigenous world, which he shared with other early Franciscan

12. Sahagún, *Introductions and Indices*, prologue to Book I, 45–46.

13. In "To the Sincere Reader" of the prologue to *Book I*, Sahagún once more reminds readers that his linguistic works in the series will contribute to the learning of Mexican language and linguistic development: "Certainly it would be very beneficial to produce so useful a work for those who desire to learn this Mexican language.... And, so, it was impossible for me to prepare a dictionary. But I have laid the groundwork in order that whoever may desire can prepare it with ease, for, through my efforts twelve Books have been written in an idiom characteristic and typical of this Mexican language... also are found therein all the manner of speech and all the words this language uses...." León-Portilla argues that Sahagún's linguistic interest, closely tied to the zeal of evangelization, was another strong motivation for the *General History*. See León-Portilla, *Sahagún: First Anthropologist*, 134–36.

historia general de las cosas de nueva españa

missionaries to New Spain, and also commanded and supported by his religious superior,[14] Sahagún embarked on the ambitious project to compile the *General History* for the evangelization of the Nahuas (prologue to *Book II*, 53). Keeping Sahagún's intention in mind, the following section will discuss his impressions of and biases against the Nahua world.

SAHAGÚN'S ATTITUDE TOWARD THE NAHUA WORLD: RELIGION, CULTURE, AND PEOPLE

Sahagún was sure that the Nahuas were vulnerable to relapsing into ancient idolatry, lured by the "devil."[15] Sahagún states that with the clear intention to prevent this, he had written the first five books, which deal with the gods, ceremonies, the origin of the gods, soothsayers, and omens respectively (prologue to *Book III*, 59). The first five books out of the twelve concentrate on "the divine, or rather idolatrous"[16] things of New Spain, and intend to provide missionaries with practical knowledge conducive to identifying pagan practices among the Nahuas.

It is apparent that Sahagún was hostile to any form of Nahua culture related to pagan religious beliefs and practices. His biased attitude toward the ancient indigenous religion is manifested in the dismissive rhetoric he adopted to describe the "the divine, or rather idolatrous" things in the five books.

Although he was unfavorable and alert to the religious beliefs and practices of the Nahuas out of concerns about idolatry, his opinion of "human things" in New Spain was quite distinguishable from that of "divine things." In the prologue to *Book I*, he acknowledges that various aspects of pre-conquest Nahua culture were worthwhile. Refuting general prejudice against the native people and their culture by the Spaniards, he recognizes

---

14. In his prologue to *Book I*, Sahagún provides the name of the prelate who ordered him to write the twelve books. The religious superior is Fray Francisco Torla, provincial of the Province of the Holy Gospel. See Sahagún, prologue to *Book I*, 46.

15. "And if one thinks that these things are so forgotten and lost and the belief in one God is established and rooted among these natives so that there will be no need at any time to speak of these matters, such a person I believe piously, but *I know of a certainty* that neither does the devil sleep nor is the reverence these natives render him forgotten; and that he is awaiting an opportunity, that he may return to the dominion he has held. And it will then be an easy matter for him to awaken all things pertaining to idolatry that are said to be forgotten." Sahagún, prologue to *Book III*, 59.

16. Sahagún, prologue to *Book I*, 46.

excellence in their administration: "They are considered as barbarians, as a people at the lowest level of perfection, when in reality (excluding some injustices their mode of governance contained) in matters of good conduct they surpass many other nations which have great confidence in their administrations" (prologue to *Book I*, 47).

He also appreciates the wealth and grandeur of the ancient civilization, mentioning Cholula, an ancient city as prosperous as Rome. Furthermore, Sahagún compares Mexico City to Venice (prologue to *Book VIII*, 69–70). And concerning the religious life of the Nahuas, while opposing the pagan worship of the Nahuas, Sahagún acknowledges their devout commitment to their gods and goddesses, which involved some burdensome religious ceremonies (prologue to *Book I*, 49).

Other virtues of the Nahuas that Sahagún considers valuable are mutual respect among the people and fortitude, which is indispensable in a society where war is taken for granted (prologue to *Book VI*, 65). In addition, Sahagún is assured of the Nahuas' ability to learn and live in the Christian faith, drawing on his eyewitness experience of the ancient civilization and his own interactions with the people. He insists, "they are no less capable of our Christianity; besides, they have been duly indoctrinated therein. It certainly seems, in our times, in these lands and with this people, that our Lord God has willed to restore to the Church that which the demon robbed her of in England, Germany, France, Asia, and Palestine" (prologue to *Book I*, 50). Here, the Franciscan zeal for the new Christian kingdom is evident.

This optimistic tone regarding the evangelization of the Nahuas and the establishment of an ideal Christian community seems contradictory to his suspicion of the idolatrous practices exercised by the same people and his concerns over what he saw as a moral collapse.[17] He was witness to the well-maintained Nahua society's collapse not only in terms of political independence, but also in the moral norms of its people. Although it was necessary, the destruction of the pre-conquest order, along with its idolatrous buildings and customs, dismantled the sustainability of moral norms among the Nahuas, which were organically interwoven with all other social systems. Sahagún regrets that the newly established order by the Spaniards produced "very licentious people of very evil tendencies and very evil works, which make them odious to God and to men, and even cause them great sicknesses and a short life" (Author's Account in *Book X*, 75).

---

17. Sahagún, prologue to *Book X*, 75–81.

In this way, Sahagún's view of Nahua world is complicated. On one hand, he is very cautious of and hostile to everything connected to idolatry, and on the other hand, he has high regard for the Nahua people's enthusiastic zeal for their religion. He wants to revive and preserve aspects of the culture that can be helpful to the indigenous people. At the same time, however, he acknowledges that valuable aspects of the culture and certain virtues are deeply connected to their religion. He sometimes seems very optimistic about the potential of the Nahua people to learn and live the Christian faith and conform to the missionaries' view of a moral life, whereas he often does not hide his disappointment at what he deems failure. Nevertheless, he never abandons hope for the people in New Spain. All these biases, thoughts, and sentiments are found in his references to the devotional practice in Tepeyac, which this paper explores going forward.

OUR LADY OF GUADALUPE IN THE GENERAL HISTORY

In Notes from *Book XI*,[18] Sahagún enumerates various locations and their idolatrous ceremonies, which the Nahuas carried out and continued to carry out post-conquest in the waters and the mountains, so as to show how the geographical features of the land of New Spain are associated with idolatry. First, he discusses lagoons, springs and other bodies of water and the religious practices there (Note in *Introductions and Indices*, 89–93). Then, he looks into three places near mountains: Tepeyac, Tlaxcalla and Tianquizmanalco. A notable point regarding the worship places in mountains is that unlike the places in waters, visitors worshipped the ancient Nahua gods under the guise of celebration of Christian saints. Sahagún first draws attention to Tepeyac where there is a temple dedicated to Our Lady of Guadalupe:

> Near the mountains, there are three or four places where they were accustomed to perform very solemn sacrifices and they came to them from very distant lands. One of these is here in Mexico where there is a small mountain they call Tepeyacac. The Spaniards call it Tepeaquilla; now it is called Nuestra Señora de Guadalupe. At this place they had a temple dedicated to the mother of the gods whom they called Tonantzin, which means Our Mother.

18. In the original Spanish version of Sahagún's *Book XI*, the notes (Note and Note Also) are added to paragraphs 6 and 7 of chapter 12 of *Book XI*. For current reference purposes, find the Note and Note Also in Sahagún, *Introductions and Indices*, 89–93.

There they performed many sacrifices in honor of this goddess. And they came to them from more than twenty leagues away, from all the border regions of Mexico, and they brought many offerings. Men and women, youths and maidens came to these feasts. There was a great conflux of people on these days, and they all said: "We are going to the feast of Tonantzin." And now that a church of Our Lady of Guadalupe is built there, they also call her Tonantzin, being motivated by the preachers who called Our Lady, the Mother of God, Tonantzin. It is not known for certain where the beginning of this Tonantzin may have originated, but this we know for certain, that, from its first usage, the word means that ancient Tonantzin. And it is something that should be remedied, for the correct [native] name of the Mother of God, Holy Mary, is not Tonantzin but rather Dios inantzin. It appears to be a Satanic invention to cloak idolatry under the confusion of this name, Tonantzin. And they now come to visit this Tonantzin from very far away, as far away as before, which is also suspicious, because everywhere there are many churches of Our Lady and they do not go to them. They come from distant lands to this Tonantzin as in olden times.[19]

Sahagún introduces two more places.[20] The second place is a temple dedicated to the ancient goddess who was called "Toci," meaning "our grandmother" in Nahuatl, and also known by another name, Tzapotlan tenan.[21] Here, the Franciscans built a church dedicated to Saint Ann along with their monastery. Sahagún suspects that the Nahua pilgrims actually visit the church to honor Tzapotlan tenan, who shares her other title of Toci with Saint Ann, in that she was the grandmother of Jesus. The third place of concern is Tianquizmanalco San Juan, where the Nahuas used to hold a great feast in honor of Tezcatlipoca, also called Telpochtli, meaning a virgin in Nahuatl. Sahagún suggests that learning from the preachers that Saint John the Evangelist was a virgin, the Nahuas associated him with Tezcatlipoca under the name of Telpochtli[22] which became the shared title for both the Christian saint and the Nahua god.

Five points are noteworthy in the description of these three places, the ancient sites of the Nahua religion made Christian shrines. First, the

19. Sahagún, Note in *Introductions and Indices*, 90.

20. For the full text referring to the two places, see the appendix at the end of this paper.

21. For more on Toci, see Sahagún, *Book I*, 17.

22. Sahagún is not sure whether the saint is Saint John the Evangelist or Baptist. See Note Also in Sahagún, *Introductions and Indices*, 92.

aim of this portion of the text is in accord with the author's general intention of writing a series of books covering almost everything pertaining to the Nahuas. In Note Also from *Book XI*, Sahagún writes, "It is clear that, in the minds of the common people who come there, it is nothing other than the ancient custom. *I now know that it comes from the ancient custom*" (Note Also in *Introductions and Indices*, 92)[23]. The main purpose of the volumes is to help the evangelizers of the Nahuas by facilitating learning of the language, and to provide necessary information on the belief, life, and environment of the native people so that they could discern the idolatrous practices concealed from them. The laborious investigation and accomplishment of what Sahagún intended in his works made him claim with confidence, "I now know."

Second, despite his suspicion of the hidden intention of the devotional pilgrimage to the allegedly Christian shrines, Sahagún does not insist that the devotional practice should be discarded as a whole. He wants to purify the religious practices from their idolatrous elements and help the pilgrims direct their vigorous devotion in the right direction, toward the Christian God and saints. He writes, "It is not my judgment that they should be denied either the coming or the offering, but it is my judgment that they be undeceived of the error from which they suffer, by giving them to understand, on those days they come there, the ancient falsehood, and that it is not as in times of old" (Note Also in *Introductions and Indices*, 92). In this regard, he suggests that the Mother of God, Holy Mary, should be called "Dios inantzin," which means "mother of God," rather than "Tonantzin" in order to distinguish Mary from the Nahua goddesses.[24]

Sahagún goes on to emphasize the prudent guidance of missionaries in helping the new Christians be "undeceived of the error from which they suffer": "Preachers well versed in the language and the ancient customs which they had, as well as in the Holy Writ, should do this." (Note Also in *Introductions and Indices*, 92). Here one can catch the missionary's complex sentiment regarding the Nahuas. While suspicious of idolatrous practices,

23. Italics are mine.

24. Sahagún identifies the Nahua goddess with Cihuacoatl. "Esta diosa se llama Cihuacoatl, que quiere decir 'mujer de la culebra'. Y también la llamaban Tonantzin, que quiere decir 'nuestra madre'. En estas dos cosas parece que esta diosa es nuestra madre Eva, la cual fue engañada de la culebra, y que ellos tenían noticia del negocio que pasó entre nuestra madre Eva y la culebra." The Spanish version is quoted in Ríos Castaño, "Domesticating the Nahuas," 219. Sahagún does not mention that Cihuacoatl is addressed as Tonantzin in the Nahuatl version, however. See Sahagún, *Book I*, 11.

he is earnestly concerned about the Nahuas' spiritual health and encourages other missionaries to work more cautiously with the hope that they would lead the Nahua people to a purer faith.

Third, Sahagún identifies the missionaries' part in the erroneous intermingling of two different religious practices. For the appellation of Tonantzin for Mary, he attributes its initiation to the friars, saying, "they also call her Tonantzin, being motivated by the preachers who called Our Lady, the Mother of God, Tonantzin" (Note in *Introductions and Indices*, 90). In a similar fashion, Sahagún argues, use of both the Nahuatl word Toci for Saint Ann and Telpochtli for Saint John were motivated by the preachers and produced the unexpected result that the native people could legitimate the continuous practice of ancient idolatry by taking advantage of the confusing names.

During the early stages of the Franciscan mission in New Spain, the Spanish Christians, missionaries and soldiers tried to destroy everything related to idolatry, such as buildings, customs, idols, and codices.[25] However, sometime around 1529, the Franciscans began to change their mission strategy toward a direction where they investigate and gather the information about the Nahua culture, religion, custom, and language in order to utilize them to gain the Indians' confidence and respect.[26] The preference of Mary as a subject of sermons was considered in this sense, for Mary, the Virgin Mother of God, could be easily compared to Coatlicue,[27] the virgin mother of Huitzilopochtli.[28] The Franciscans not only purposefully related the pagan deities and their names to Christian ones; they also allowed the native Nahuas to involve religious items and customs such as dancing, songs, the offering of flowers, costumes, decoration of the church, etc. These cultural elements, like those mentioned above, were not totally separated from pagan practices and beliefs, which the Nahuas still could

---

25. "Author's Account Worthy of Being Noted," in Sahagún, *Book X*, 75; Kroger and Granziera, *Aztec Goddesses*, 137.

26. Kroger and Granziera, *Aztec Goddesses*, 136–37.

27. Sahagún identifies Tonantzin with Cihuacoatl, who is the highest of the goddesses. See Note Also in *Introductions and Indices*, 92; Book I, Ch. 6 and 11. On the other hand, *Book III*, "The Origin of the Gods," presents a goddess named Coatlicue as the virgin mother of the god of the Sun, Huitzilopochtli (or Uitzilopochtli). See Sahagún, *Book III: The Origin of the Gods*, 16.

28. Kroger and Granziera, *Aztec Goddesses*, 138.

recognize even in the Christianized forms.[29] Joseph Kroger and Patrizia Granziera summarize the Franciscan tactics of evangelization as follows:

> This mingling of pagan practices with Christian ones was possible because the friars believed that while the form of these spectacles was necessary to attract and keep the attention of the Indians, it was their content (written or adapted by the friars) that was the real means of conversion. Once the attention of the indigenous population was captured, the moral and religious lessons taught in the plays would persuade them to abandon their pagan beliefs.[30]

Sahagún does not totally reject the adaptation of the religious concepts and culture from the pre-conquest Nahua world, which he considers necessary in order to more effectively guide the Nahuas to Christian belief.[31] Nevertheless, as mentioned previously, he was very cautious about the possibility that the neophytes could take advantage of the syncretistic tactics with the intention of concealing pagan practices and beliefs. When Sahagún writes that the Christian preachers motivated the association of the Nahua deities' names with Christian saints, he adds criticism of the mission tactic implemented by the Franciscans who "deliberately remained silent" of and "consciously allowed"[32] the religious syncretism. Sahagún argues that, in the end, this attitude hindered missionaries from properly Christianizing and disciplining the Nahuas.

An attempt to demythologize the Nahuas' religious beliefs is prevalent throughout the *General History*, as apparent in the fourth noteworthy point in Sahagún's depiction of the three worship places: his explanation of how the religious phenomena relate to the geographical environment. He offers a scientific elucidation to the question of why these places became the destination of religious pilgrimage to which the native people gravitate, not even sparing themselves from walking from distant lands:

> And the attachment which this people adopted anciently to coming to visit these places is [from this]; since these indicated mountains spontaneously produce clouds which constantly rain in certain areas, the people who live in those lands where these clouds which form in these mountains shower, observing that the benefaction of rain comes to them from those mountains, considered themselves

---

29. Ibid., 137–45.
30. Ibid., 143.
31. Morales, "Native Encounter," 137–59.
32. Kroger and Granziera, *Aztec Goddesses*, 144.

obligated to go to visit those places and give thanks to that divinity which resided there, which sent the water, and to take their offerings in appreciation for the benefaction which they received therefrom.... in Mexico in the feast of Cioacoatl who is also called Tonantzin, in Tlaxcalla in the feast of Toçi, in Tianquizmanalco in the feast of Tezcatlipoca.[33]

The mountain was an important landscape in the symbolism of the Nahua cosmology and mythology. It was identified as the pregnant belly of Mother Earth, and caves in mountains were considered the portal to the goddess. Mountains were also essential to the life of the Nahuas since the sources of water—all rivers, springs, and rain proceeded from mountains. Because of that, the Nahuas believed that mountains represent powerful goddesses who are in control of water.[34]

Finally, the fifth point pertains to the absence of reported miracles at the three devotional sites. Miracles played a significant role in attracting pilgrims to Christian sanctuaries in sixteenth-century New Spain. But in the case of the Saint Ann site, Sahagún argues, "also in this place, idolatry appears to be cloaked because so many people come from such distant lands without Saint Ann's ever having performed any miracles there"(Note in *Introductions and Indices*, 91). For Tianquizmanalco San Juan too, he is wary of the real intention of pilgrimage since "Saint John has performed no miracles there, neither is there reason to meet there rather than any other place where he has a church" (Note in *Introductions and Indices*, 91).

Sahagún does not apply this logic to the case of Our Lady of Guadalupe in Tepeyac, however. Yet with no mention of miracles, he still questions the real intention of the Nahuas' pilgrimage to Tepeyac rather than to many other churches built in honor of Mary. Comparing the logic utilized in Sahagún's arguments in the three cases, it should be noted that there actually occurred many miracles in Tepeyac. If no miracles had occurred at all in Tepeyac, Sahagún may have argued that despite no miracles, the Nahuas persisted in visiting Tepeyac for suspicious reasons, as he does for other two places. Then why does Sahagún not make reference at all to the miracles in Tepeyac? The answer may lie in that the Franciscans wanted to build the Indian Church by doctrine and their exemplary life of poverty and simplicity. They thought that too many miracles and supernatural events might facilitate relapse of the new converts into superstitions and

33. Sahagún, Note Also in *Introductions and Indices*, 92.
34. Kroger and Granziera, *Aztec Goddesses*, 36–39; Lara, *City, Temple, Stage*, 91–94.

historia general de las cosas de nueva españa

idolatry, preventing them from a firm and sound faith.³⁵ The silence about miracles in Tepeyac may indeed imply this caution.

This paper examined Sahagún's references to Guadalupe in light of the general purpose of the *General History*, his thoughts on the Franciscan mission, and his ambivalent attitude toward Nahua culture as revealed in prologues and notes to the twelve books. The short but significant text does not remain a mere evidence of the historicity of Guadalupe phenomena. In the written witness of a Franciscan missionary who observed early religious practices surrounding Guadalupe, one sees an intricate mind that contemplated the Marian devotion from a complex viewpoint. Sahagún was suspicious about the syncretic devotion, but didn't discard it as a whole. He pointed out the hidden pagan intention of the pilgrims to the Christian shrines, but he also admitted the responsibility of missionaries in part. Most of all, his clear intention in writing his brief passage on Guadalupe and two other Christian devotions was evangelical. He wanted the readers, in particular the missionaries, to be well acquainted with the nature of current religious practices and make efforts to purify them. All these points are made clearer when the text is read with a broad understanding of the *General History*.

APPENDIX: PART OF NOTE AND THE ENTIRE NOTE ALSO FROM BOOK XI, IN INTRODUCTIONS AND INDICES³⁶

Near the mountains, there are three or four places where they were accustomed to perform very solemn sacrifices and they came to them for very distant lands. One of these is here in Mexico where there is a small mountain they call Tepeyacac. The Spaniards call it Tepeaquilla; now is called Nuestra Señora de Guadalupe. At this place they had a temple dedicated to the mother of the gods whom they called Tonantzin, which means Our Mother. There they performed many sacrifices in honor of this goddess. And they came to them from more than twenty leagues away, from all the border regions of Mexico, and they brought many offerings. Men and women, youths and maidens came to these feasts. There was a great conflux

---

35. On the other hand, the paucity of miracles was questioned since the Franciscan friars compared the Indian church to the primitive church in the Apostolic Era, during which the apostles worked many miracles. Leddy Phelan, *Millennial Kingdom*, 50–51.

36. Sahagún, *Introductions and Indices*, 90–93.

of people on these days, and they all said: "We are going to the feast of Tonantzin." And now that a church of Our Lady of Guadalupe is built there, they also call her Tonantzin, being motivated by the preachers who called Our Lady, the Mother of God, Tonantzin. It is not known for certain where the beginning of this Tonantzin may have originated, but this we know for certain, that, from its first usage, the word means that ancient Tonantzin. And it is something that should be remedied, for the correct [native] name of the Mother of God, Holy Mary, is not Tonantzin but rather Dios inantzin. It appears to be a Satanic invention to cloak idolatry under the confusion of this name, Tonantzin. And they now come to visit this Tonantzin from very far away, as far away as before, which is also suspicious, because everywhere there are many churches of Our Lady and they do not go to them. They come from distant lands to this Tonantzin as in olden times.

The second place where there were anciently many sacrifices, to which they came from distant lands, is near the mountain range of Tlaxcalla where there was a temple which was called Toci, where a great multitude of people met at the celebration of this feast. Toci means Our Grandmother, and by another name she was called Tzapotlan tenan, which means the goddess of sweatbaths and medicines. And subsequently they built a church of Santa Ana there, where there is now a monastery with monks of Our Father Saint Francis. And the natives call her Toci, and people from over forty leagues away attend the feast of Toci. And they name Santa Ana in this manner, being motivated by the preachers who say that, since Santa Ana is the grandmother of Jesus Christ she is also our grandmother, [grandmother] of all Christians. And so they have called her and call her Toci at the pulpit, which means our grandmother. And all the people who come, as in times past, to the feast of Toci, come on the pretext of Saint Ann. But since the word is ambiguous, and they respect the olden ways, it is believable that they come more for the ancient than for the modern. And thus, also in this place, idolatry appears to be cloaked because so many people come from such distant lands without Saint Ann's ever having performed any miracles there. It is more apparent that it is the ancient Toci rather than Saint Ann. In this year of 1576 the plague which prevails began there and, they say, there are no people there now. It seems mysterious for the punishment to have started there where the transgression of cloaking idolatry under the name of Saint Ann started.

The third place where there were anciently many sacrifices, to which they came from distant lands, is at the foot of the volcano, in a village of

Calpa, which is called Tianquizmanalco San Juan. At this place, they performed a great feast in honor of the god they called Telpochtli which is Tezcalipoca. And as they heard the preachers say that Saint John the Evangelist was a virgin, and such in their language is called *telpochtli*, they took occasion to perform that feast as they were accustomed to perform it in times past, cloaked under the name of San Juan Telpochtli as it appears on the surface but [performed] in honor of the old Telpochtli, which is Tezcatlipoca. Since Saint John has performed no miracles there, neither is there reason to meet there rather than any other place where he has a church.

Note Also

Nowadays great numbers of people from very distant lands come to this feast and they bring many offerings. And with regard to this, it is similar to the ancient ways although they do not practice the sacrifices and cruelties which they practiced anciently. And [as to] their having practiced this dissimulation in these aforementioned places, I am well assured in my judgment that they do not do it out of love for the idols but rather out of love for avarice and ostentation, so that the offerings which used to be customary should not be lost, nor the glory of ostentation which they received by these places being visited by many strange people from distant lands.

And the attachment which this people adopted anciently to coming to visit these places is [from this]; since these indicated mountains spontaneously produce clouds which constantly rain in certain areas, the people who live in those lands where these clouds which form in these mountains shower, observing that the benefaction of rain comes to them from those mountains, considered themselves obligated to go to visit those places and give thanks to that divinity which resided there, which sent the water, and to take their offerings in appreciation for the benefaction which they received therefrom. And so the dwellers of those lands which were sprinkled by the clouds of those mountains, persuaded or threatened by the demon or his agents, adopted the custom and attachment to come to visit those mountains each year in the feast which was assigned there: in Mexico in the feast of Cioacoatl who is also called Tonantzin, in Tlaxcalla in the feast of Toçi, in Tianquizmanalco in the feast of Tezcatlipoca.

And, in order that they not lose this custom, the villages that enjoyed it persuaded those provinces that they come as usual because they already had Tonantzin and Tocitzin and Telpochtli, who on the surface were like, or whom they made like, Saint Mary, Saint Ann, and Saint John the Evangelist or Baptist. And it is clear that, in the minds of the common people who come there, it is nothing other than the ancient custom. I now know that it comes from ancient custom. And it is not my judgment that they should be denied either the coming or the offering, but it is my judgment that they be undeceived of the error from which they suffer, by giving them to understand, on those days they come there, the ancient falsehood, and that it is not as in times of old. Preachers well versed in the language and the ancient customs which they had, as well as in the Holy Writ, should do this.

I verily believe that there are many other places in these Indies where reverence and offerings to the idols are clandestinely practiced under the pretext of the feasts which the Church celebrates to revere God and His saints. It would be good that such be investigated, that the poor people be undeceived of the error from which they now suffer.

BIBLIOGRAPHY

Brading, D. A. *Mexican Phoenix: Our Lady of Guadalupe; Image and Tradition Across Five Centuries*. Cambridge: Cambridge University Press, 2001.

Kroger, Joseph and Patrizia Granziera. *Aztec Goddesses and Christian Madonnas: Images of the Divine Feminine in Mexico*. Burlington, VT: Ashgate, 2012.

Lara, Jaime. *City, Temple, Stage: Eschatological Architecture and Liturgical Theatrics in New Spain*. Notre Dame, IN: University of Notre Dame Press, 2004.

Leddy Phelan, John. *The Millennial Kingdom of the Franciscans in the New World*. Berkeley: University of California Press, 1970.

León-Portilla, Miguel. *Bernardino de Sahagún: First Anthropologist*. Translated by Mauricio J. Mixco. Norman: University of Oklahoma Press, 2002.

———. "Significado de la obra de Fray Bernardino de Sahagún," *Estudios de Historia Novohispana*. 1 (1966) 21.

Morales, Francisco. "The Native Encounter with Christianity: Franciscans and Nahuas in Sixteenth-Century Mexico." *The Americas* 65.2 (2008).

Poole, Stafford. *Our Lady of Guadalupe: The Origins and Sources of a Mexican National Symbol, 1531–1797*. Tucson: University of Arizona Press, 1995.

Ríos Castaño, Victoria. "Domesticating the Nahuas: Sahagún's Cultural Translation of Nahua Gods and Ceremonies in Book I of *Historia universal de las cosas de Nueva España*." *Romance Studies* 27.3 (2009) 219.

Sahagún, Bernardino de. *Florentine Codex: General History of the Things of New Spain, Introductions and Indices* and *Books I–XII*. Translated by Arthur J. O. Anderson and Charles E. Dibble. Santa Fe, NM: The School of American Research and The University of Utah, 1982.

2

"May You Be Joyful, Oh Saint Mary"
Translating and Transforming Marian Devotion in New Spain

Katharine Mahon

> Beloved one, beloved person of distinction, Christian, beloved spiritual son, recognize [and] pay honor to your spiritual chaplet of flowers; to the cloth with a number of different necklaces of radiating pendants, to your flowery paper, with which your mother holy Church adorns you. It is made of a number of surpassingly perfect flowers glistening like gold and precious jade, spreading their light. These are the Ave Maria and the Salve Regina. Lady, Saint Mary, I greet you. May you be happy. You are full of grace. The Lord is with you. As one who is blessed, you exceed all women who have lived and who will live. Noble are your vestments in which our Lord God has clothed you. And as for the jewel, the quetzal feather of your womb, Jesus, Who came to your bosom, surpassingly noble are His vestments, His adornment. You who are virgin, who are Saint Mary, who are ever virgin, who are God's mother, pray for us sinners, intercede for us before God now and at the threshold of our death. This is the prayer with which God's beloved mother, Saint Mary, is prayed to. It lies written in the holy Gospel. Each word is a flower [of the chaplet] with which we make an offering to the Lady, Saint Mary.[1]

This discourse on Marian prayer, written by sixteenth century Franciscan missionary to Mexico Bernardino de Sahagún, appears in the prologue of his *Psalmodia Christiana*, a book of Christian psalmody in Nahuatl for the

---

1. Sahagún, *Psalmodia Christiana*, 23–25.

native to sing throughout the liturgical year. Embedded within the flowery, image-laden language, one can discern the general outline of the archetypal Marian prayer—the *Ave Maria*. The *Ave Maria* here, however, is not a mere translation of the Latin prayer into Nahuatl; here the prayer is distinctly transformed, translated not just into the tongue of the native Nahua inhabitants of New Spain, but into the Nahua literary style and culture itself. This excerpt represents—with its use of Nahua speech patterns, jewel and flower imagery, and sacrificial language—perhaps the best example of a sixteenth-century attempt to inculturate Christian Marian devotion into the Nahua context. Not a mere translation of Sahagún's thoughts into Nahuatl, as explained by the *Psalmodia's* modern English translator, Arthur J.O. Anderson, the *Psalmodia* was an endeavor to replace the popular practice of "profane" Nahuatl songs and dances with Christian versions. Imitating the style of these songs, the *Psalmodia's* compositions notably utilized "The device of rich, repetitious enumeration of kinds of precious flowers, of precious stones, and of precious capes [which was] typical of the old days."[2]

In teaching the newly converted Nahuas the fundamentals of Christian worship and piety, the missionaries to New Spain—first the Franciscans, then the Augustinians, Dominicans, and Jesuits—drew upon the rich tradition of European Marian devotions in order to instruct the neophytes in practicing their new faith in worship and devotion. Yet, as can be seen in any successful missionary setting, the faith of the missionaries must first be adapted to the new cultural context before new manifestations of the faith can appear and grow among the converted population. Translation of the important texts, prayers, and practices is merely the first step in this missionary process. This essay will explore the missionaries' early efforts at teaching Marian theology, devotion, and prayer to their Nahua flocks during the colonial period, from the conquest in 1519 until the 1649 publication of the *Nican mopohua* in Luis Laso de la Vega's *Huei tlamahuiçoltica*. Drawing upon evidence found in sermons, songs, and catechetical manuals translated from their original Nahuatl, as well as from other documentary evidence which describes liturgical, devotional, and cultural practices, we will examine both explicit teachings and implicit modeling of Marian prayer and devotion in the missionaries' works and, where possible, consider evidence of native reception of their Marian catechesis. As we will see, analysis of this devotional formation reveals two trends: on the one hand, there was an ongoing process of adapting European Marian traditions,

---

2. Anderson, "'San Bernadino,'" 109.

devotions, and prayers for Nahua usage and, on the other hand, a more complicated process of teaching doctrine and correcting misconceptions about the Blessed Virgin Mary to the Nahua while also encouraging genuine love and devotion to Mary among them.

The text of Sahagún's *Psalmodia*, which was likely begun in the 1550s and finally published in 1583,[3] chronologically follows decades after the traditional dating of the Guadalupan event of 1531. The Marian-themed works of Sahagún and the other missionaries which will be discussed in this essay, however, antedate the extant textual evidence of missionary teaching about Our Lady of Guadalupe, which begins with the publication of the *Nican mopohua*—the first Nahuatl account of the events at Tepeyac—in 1649 and grows exponentially afterwards. The sixteenth and early-seventeenth century texts used for this research, then, while concurrent with—and perhaps foundational for—the beginnings of catechetical works on Guadalupan devotion for the Nahua, are considered pre-Guadalupan as they are representative of the missionary efforts and Marian piety which pre-dates the proliferation of Guadalupan-focused Marian devotion of New Spain from the seventeenth century onwards. Thus, while Nahua devotion to Our Lady of Guadalupe likely grew during the period covered in this essay, the lack of any extant Nahuatl texts about Guadalupe (written by missionaries) before the *Nican mopohua* means that extant textual referents to Guadalupe in Nahua Marian devotion before Luis Laso de la Vega's *Huei tlamahuiçoltica* are limited to observations about ritual and devotional practices.

This work is deeply indebted to the work of Louise M. Burkhart, whose book, *Before Guadalupe: The Virgin Mary in Early Colonial Nahuatl Literature*, provides the bulk of the evidence for Marian devotion and catechesis which will be discussed, and, without whose indispensible translations and invaluable commentary, this essay would not have been possible. While Burkhart organizes her work according to Marian devotional themes (her conception, assumption, prayers, miracle narratives, etc.), this essay will proceed chronologically as well as thematically. We will first situate ourselves in the pre-missionary and early missionary context in relation to Marian devotion: the state of Marian catechesis and pious practices among the Nahua which the earliest missionaries to New Spain had to contend with. Then, we will move to Marian liturgical feasts (communal ecclesial celebrations of Mary), followed by Marian prayers (private and personal devotion to Mary), as explicated and demonstrated in missionary sermons

---

3. Anderson, "San Bernadino," 108.

of the sixteenth century. As the decades following the conquest progressed, the Spanish missionaries increasingly utilized native culture in their catechetical and devotional endeavors; the fourth section of this essay will explore the missionaries' processes of translating the language and practices of Marian devotion into Nahuatl and Nahua culture. Finally, we will turn our attention to the seventeenth century, when missionaries began to turn their catechetical attention to a flourishing native Marian devotion—Our Lady of Guadalupe. As we explore these topics, I will argue that, through their efforts to transform native conceptions of Mary and translate Old World Marian devotions into authentic New World piety, the missionaries of New Spain laid the foundations for widespread Nahua Marian devotion and the growth of devotion to Guadalupe among native believers.

"THE CONQUERING VIRGIN": PRE-MISSIONARY CONCEPTIONS OF MARY IN NAHUA THOUGHT

For most of the Nahuas during the Spanish conquest, their introduction to Christianity did not begin with Jesus Christ, but with his mother, the Blessed Virgin Mary. As Joseph Kroger and Patrizia Granziera explain in their book *Aztec Goddesses and Christian Madonnas*, from the very beginning Mary was central to Nahua conceptions of the conquistadors' religion: "While a methodical approach to conversion did not begin until after the arrival of Franciscan missionaries in 1524, the first experience that the Indians had of the image of Mary was in their encounter with the conquistadors five years earlier."[4] As a result of their own religion, which featured a war goddess who was also the Mother of God, and the influence of the conquistadors' emblematic use of Marian imagery in battle, for the Nahua "images of Mary were associated with war and conquest from the moment the Spaniards set foot on the shores of Mexico."[5] Mary was, moreover, conceived in the Nahua mind as the principle divinity of Christianity, no doubt exacerbated by the Spaniards' own Marian maximalism. Hernán Cortés was famously devoted to Mary; he, like most Spaniards, purportedly carried her image with him at all times. In one telling incident, after he had defeated them in battle the day before, Cortés forced Nahua chiefs, as well as the battle's survivors and women and children, to venerate an image

---

4. Kroger and Granziera, *Aztec Goddesses*, 128.
5. Ibid.

of *Nuestra Señora* and give up their old gods.[6] The Spaniards' allegiance to Mary and continued military successes, moreover, seemed to prove the power of Mary's favor; some accounts of Spanish-native combat include testimony, from Spaniards and Nahua alike, that told of Mary appearing to not only lead the Spanish in battle, but to even throw dirt in the eyes of the Nahua warriors, obscuring their vision and contributing to their defeat.[7]

> It is understandable, then, that when they experienced the Conquering Virgin and were told of the mother of God's supremacy, the Indians of Mexico would consider Mary, whose image they were forced to worship, a war goddess. We know that after the conquest, when Christian evangelization began in earnest, the first missionaries discovered that Mary was not only regarded as a goddess, but that the name Mary was the only name the Indians knew to designate the God of Christianity.[8]

In one sense, it seems incredible that any native devotion to Mary ever developed, considering how "the Indians' first encounter with Mary occurred in the context of death, defeat and humiliation at the hands of her devotees."[9]

Although some priests accompanied the first wave of conquistadors, their work in Mexico was largely limited to ministry to the Spaniards. The evangelization of the natives, then, was left in the hands of the conquering soldiers, whose methods of forced worship and minimal explanation were strongly objected to by the priests who accompanied them.[10] It was not until the first Franciscan missionaries arrived in New Spain in 1524, five years after the beginning of the conquest, that any sweeping corrective evangelization and catechetical measures were undertaken for the sake of the native population. Through sermons, catechetical instruction, prayer, and example, the missionaries began the work of re-presenting Mary to the Nahua: Mary as the mother of Christ, not Christ himself; Mary as dear mother, not a ruthless war goddess; Mary as the intercessor of all the faithful, not the powerful patroness of the conquistadors; and, most importantly, the Nahua themselves as the beloved devotees of Mary, not as vanquished subjects of a *Conquistadora*. Louise Burkhart explains: "It was

6. Ibid.
7. Ibid., 131.
8. Ibid., 133.
9. Ibid., 128.
10. Ibid., 134–35.

the friars, foremost among them the Franciscans, who really brought the Nahuas into the Marian fold, and their chronicles tell their version of the story."[11] A number of primary sources attest that, in the decades that followed, Mary continued to occupy a prominent place in the conversion of the native population to Christianity. The efforts of the first Franciscan missionaries and those of other orders who followed, however, were directed less towards introducing converts to Mary than to *re*introducing them to Mary: correcting their misconceptions and transforming their relationship to her through sermons and catechesis, liturgical celebrations and communal worship, and private prayer and devotion.

CELEBRATING MARY: SERMONS AND CELEBRATIONS THROUGHOUT THE LITURGICAL YEAR

Liturgical feasts of Mary, spaced throughout the weeks and seasons of the liturgical year, were a central means of conveying the importance of Mary in salvation history while placing her within the larger context of Christ's life, death, and resurrection. The requirements of Mass attendance on any Marian-themed Holy Days of obligation, moreover, served to reaffirm her considerable role in the life of the Church and also guaranteed larger audiences for preachers who felt the need to clarify Marian theology or promote devotion related to the day's celebration. A full one-third of the twelve holy days of obligation for the Nahuas in New Spain were Marian in theme or custom—the feasts of the Purification on February 2nd, the Annunciation on March 25th, the Assumption on August 15th, and the Nativity of Mary on September 8th.[12] The feast of Mary's Conception on December 8th—celebrated as her *immaculate* conception in practice if not yet officially in Catholic doctrine—also loomed large in the liturgical year.

The surviving Nahuatl-language sermons by European missionaries on Mary, many of which Louise Burkhart has compiled in her book *Before Guadalupe*, for the most part follow the pattern of the Marian feasts of the liturgical year. The missionaries' sermons—preached on the day of the feast they commemorate, if not during the Mass itself[13]—usually re-

---

11. Burkhart, *Before Guadalupe*, 3.

12. Ibid.

13. Unlike the rubrics of the modern Roman Catholic Mass, there was no fixed point in the Mass for the sermon in the Middle Ages or the Early Modern period. Sermons certainly could have followed the Gospel readings and preceded the celebration of the

counted either the Gospel reading in Nahuatl or the corresponding lesson for the feast. The Purification of Mary almost always featured the scene of the Presentation of Christ in the Temple from Luke's Gospel, but often included theological discussions of the necessity of Mary observing the Law concerning the purification of women despite her sinlessness, purity, and ongoing virginity *in partu* and post-partum. The Annunciation sermons likewise recounted the scene of the Annunciation from the first chapter of the Gospel of Luke. Sermons on the feasts of the Assumption, Nativity of Mary, and Immaculate Conception, however, almost invariably narrated the stories of Mary's Assumption (in the case of the Assumption) and of her childhood from the *Protoevangelium of James* (in the case of Mary's Nativity and Conception). The *Protoevangelium* features Mary's miraculous conception—her parents, Joachim and Anna being hitherto barren in the vein of Abraham and Sarah and Zechariah and Elizabeth—and her wonder-filled and cloistered childhood follows along the same lines of the centuries-old tradition. Conversely, the accounts of her Assumption reflect the fluid nature of the theology of Mary's Assumption at that point in its development.

The popularity of these Marian feasts among the Nahua is difficult to determine. One sermon on the feast of the Purification uses the occasion to moralize the popular Candlemas procession, explaining to those gathered that their souls should shine forth holiness like the candles which they held brightened the darkness of night, and that sin would cloud their light.[14] Candlemas processions, complete with blessed candles for the faithful to take home with them, were very popular among the laity in Europe; given the feast's status as a Holy Day of obligation, the added elements of pageantry and participation of a procession, and the gift of a blessed object for the home, apparently the feast was popular among the Nahua faithful as well. The extant sermonic evidence does not provide any more examples of the popularity of Marian liturgical feasts, but the widespread prevalence of Assumption imagery in Marian art and its popularity in Nahua theater,[15] the overwhelming dominance of devotion to the Immaculate Conception in New Spain (albeit among the Spanish),[16] as well as the commemoration of Our Lady of Guadalupe of Extremadura on the Feast of

---

Eucharistic liturgy, but they also could have taken place immediately before or after Mass, or in the afternoon, hours after the morning Mass in celebration of the feast.

14. De la Anunciación, "Sermonario," in Burkhart, *Before Guadalupe*, 64–67.
15. Burkhart, *Before Guadalupe*, 100.
16. Ibid., 9.

the Nativity of Mary,[17] all speak to just how prominent the celebrations of these liturgical feasts and their themes must have been in the lives of the Nahua faithful. As discussed, the imagery and liturgies of the feasts of the Purification, Annunciation, Assumption, Nativity, and Immaculate Conception of Mary seem to be mere transplantations of European traditions of celebrating these feasts. Roman Catholic liturgies of the sixteenth century, however—celebrated in Latin, tightly controlled by rubrics and liturgical law (especially after the Council of Trent), and inherently more of the realm of the educated clergy than the illiterate laity (be it in Rome, Spain, or New Spain)—were not easily given over to any forms of popular adaptation. Private prayers and devotional practices, in contrast, thrive upon popular appropriations and adaptations to new contexts, and the situation of Marian piety in New Spain is a clear example of this.

PRAYING TO MARY: PIOUS DEVOTIONS AND PRACTICES

As displayed previously in Bernardino de Sahagún's remarkable adaptation of the *Ave Maria*, the missionaries of New Spain did not finish the work of devotional inculturation with mere translations of the words of prayers; translations of the language of devotion and relationship to God, Christ, and Mary needed to occur as well. Early translations and explanations of Marian prayers—the *Ave Maria* and *Salve Regina*—as well as Marian devotional practices—such as the Rosary and the similarly-structured "Crown of Saint Mary"[18]—survive from the 1550s and are featured in Burkhart's chapter on Marian prayer.[19] Undoubtedly the missionaries taught these and other Marian prayer texts and forms to the Nahua much earlier than this extant documentary evidence suggests. Both pictorial catechisms and plainsong arrangements were used early on in the missionary effort to teach the Nahua those most basic prayers which, according to the tradition of Christian formation, also constituted the most basic elements of the Christian faith:[20] the *Pater Noster, Ave Maria*, the sign of the cross, the Apostles' Creed, the *Salve Regina*, and the Ten Commandments.[21] While Protestant

17. Poole, *Our Lady of Guadalupe*, 60.
18. See description below.
19. See Burkhart, *Before Guadalupe*, 115–30.
20. See Tanner and Watson, "Least of the Laity," 395–423.
21. Burkhart, *Before Guadalupe*, 116.

reformers would critique this method of religious education as mere rote memorization by the unlettered laity without their comprehension of the faith, modern scholars have criticized its use in New Spain as an attempt to "win less the hearts and minds than the knees of the . . . Indians."[22] In their estimation, such liturgical formation—formation of the Christian by means of prayer and liturgical participation—was in fact an instrument of ensuring the barest compliance of the native "Christians" in ecclesial obligations for the sake of an ongoing "spiritual conquest" of the native population that followed upon the heels of the Spanish conquest. In the words of Richard Trexler, "The success of that [spiritual] conquest would be measured not by the assimilation of ideas but by the natives' physical and verbal comportment, which was called 'devotion.'"[23] Of course, what such critics fail to recognize is the basic catechetical and formational power of liturgical and devotional participation. Ideally, of course, all of the faithful (both in sixteenth-century New Spain and in any other time and place) would fully comprehend the tenets of the faith, be able to discuss theological topics in-depth, have a robust personal spiritual life as well as participate in a faith community, and live out their Christian faith in word and deed. But few Christians have ever attained such heights of spiritual integrity for long—usually such members of the Church are honored with the title of "saint." Given the myriad constraints of medieval Christianity (particularly concerning systematic catechesis, poor literacy rates, and lack of access to written works for even the literate), the catechetical emphasis on prayer and participation in the sacraments suggests an understanding of the role of relationship (to God, Christ, Mary, the saints, and the Church), emotion, storytelling, personal reflection, and communal identity in Christian formation. Unsurprisingly, then, while the attempt to transform the Nahua relationship with Mary is discernable in the sermons of the missionaries on Marian prayer and devotion (as noted in the introduction), evidence of attempts to form the natives through their devotional practices can also be detected.

As Burkhart explains in her chapter on Marian prayer, the inclusion of prayers in the friars' sermons seems to fulfill a variety of needs:

> Praying to Mary was, on the one hand, a devotional exercise aimed at spiritual transcendence and fulfillment, the development of

22. Trexler, *Church and Community*, 580.
23. Ibid.

an empathic identification with her and, through her, with God. On the other hand, it had the more pragmatic end of "asking for things," of enlisting Mary's help by plying her with praise and provoking her inexhaustible pity. Because prayers speak in the first person and directly to Mary, they model—more overtly than homiletic discourses—how Christian Nahuas were to interact with this principal saint.[24]

The texts of prayers were taught, yes, but so too was the Christian practice of prayer—as meditative, reflective, and relational, as well as intercessory and supplicatory. Rote prayers serve, moreover, as models of prayer, if not for memorization and personal use, then as examples that devotees could imitate in their own private prayers.

One sermon from Fray Pedro de Gante published in 1553 features the two most common Marian prayers, the *Ave Maria* and *Salve Regina*, framed by de Gante as a dialogue between a student and a teacher.

> Then we will greet our precious mother, Saint Mary, with Saint Gabriel's greeting, which is: *Ave maria gratia plena dominus tecum. Benedicta tu in muleribus. Et benedictus fructus vestrus tui Jesus. Sancta Maria virgo mater dei: ora pro nobis peccatoribus. Amen.* You do not understand these Latin words. Let us say it in our own words. May you be joyful, oh Saint Mary, you are full of grace. The ruler, God, is with you. You are the most praiseworthy of all women. And very praiseworthy is your womb of precious fruit, Jesus. Oh Saint Mary, oh perfect maiden, you are the mother of God. May you speak for us sinners. May it so be done.[25]

The explanation of the *Salve Regina*, similarly structured in Latin with the Nahuatl translation, follows. In the same manuscript, de Gante also includes a rhythmic prayer practice (not unlike the Rosary)[26] which he calls "the Crown of Saint Mary,"[27] a prayer of intercession to Mary to be said in times of illness and the danger of death,[28] and an extended oration, perhaps meant to model more personal prayer, which incorporates greetings and titles for Mary, as well as *Ave Marias* and *Pater Nosters*.[29] Little

---

24. Burkhart, *Before Guadalupe*, 115.
25. de Gante, "Doctrina Cristiana," in Burkhart, *Before Guadalupe*, 117.
26. See Graef, *Mary: A History*, 181–82.
27. Burkhart, *Before Guadalupe*, 120.
28. Ibid., 121.
29. Ibid., 119.

beyond mere translation of European prayers seems to be at play in these early sermons, interesting as the translations themselves are, as will be discussed shortly. As far as the model of devotion displayed in these sermons, the typical medieval European forms of address and self-reference appear; affectionate language is used to speak of Mary—she is called "our precious mother"[30]—and the usual doctrinal assertions—Mary's perfection, Mary's role as intercessor, Mary as queen and ever-virgin—are present, as well as the usual intercessory tropes—the devotee is painted as "wretched" and "a very big sinner."[31]

A 1565 sermon by Fray Domingo de la Anunciación features an extended explanation of the Rosary, which is translated as "Golden Flower Necklace," and described as not only a way to praise and serve Mary, but also a means to "merit many pardons." It is, most interestingly, also treated as not only an alternative to the 150 psalms, which the friars themselves sang in the Divine Office, but also as a "wondrous" means of conveying "the great wonders of our rescue," that is, the story of salvation wrought by Christ as recounted in the Gospels and Christian Tradition. De la Anunciación then proceeds to explain how to pray the Rosary and gives a point-by-point explanation of all 15 of the joyful, "painful" (sorrowful), and "happy" (glorious) mysteries, along with unique prayers to add to each mystery for further contemplation of them.[32] These descriptions are somewhat astonishing: the Rosary is presented as a devotional tool with which the devotee can honor Mary and pray in a manner similar to the friars. But, beyond pious devotion and clerical imitation, the Rosary was also seen as a means to recount and understand the events of the Gospels. The friars intended that the Rosary not only revolutionize the liturgical formation of the laity, but also serve as a great aid to the missionaries who sought to teach the Nahua neophytes the basics of Christian doctrine and train them in the methods of Christian worship.

Later sermons on Marian prayer featured in Burkhart include two orations, or long poetic prayers addressed to Mary, likely written by the friars who preached them. Such prayers do not easily lend themselves to memorization and repetitive prayer, like the Rosary or the *Ave Maria* and *Salve Regina*. These prayers do, however, model for the Nahua audiences how one should relate to Mary in prayer: terms of address and titles for Mary, clear

30. Ibid., 117.
31. Ibid., 117–21.
32. De la Anunciación, "Doctrina Xpiana," 123–27.

distinctions between the role of Mary and the role of Christ, and proper types of requests for her intercession. "You are the honored and precious daughter of God the father. You are the honored and precious mother of God the child. You are the precious and proper wife of God the Holy Spirit. You are the honored and precious temple of the most holy Trinity. May you house us little poor ones with your hands," writes Fray Juan Bautista in an oration published in 1606.[33] Mary here is deliberately described as "honored and precious" on account of her relationship—as child, mother, and spouse—to the Trinity. Through the means of her intimate relationship with God, moreover, Mary is then able to protect, favor, and intercede for her devotees. An oration by Fray Juan de Mijangos, published a year later in 1607, further explains these theological distinctions concerning Mary's intercession:

> You are the compassionate mother. May you help me and have compassion for me, may you speak for me before your precious child, our lord Jesus Christ. May you beseech him that he garland us with the various things that make one good, that make one proper, the way he garlanded you. And may you ask him to help us, so that we will scorn and abhor earthliness, the way that you despised it. And may you beseech him that he dress us preciously, with his honored mantle, his honored and sacred light, his grace, so that we will be able to serve him on earth, so that we will be able to do penance, we will weep, we will be sad on account of our sins . . . Therefore (oh precious noblewoman), by means of your honored advocacy, your help, we will obtain, we will be given heavenliness, utter joyfulness, glory.[34]

Here devotees are instructed, by example, not just to ask Mary to (ask Christ to) make them holy, but to make them holy *in the way that Mary herself was holy*. They seek to be gifted with Mary's virtues of goodness and propriety, portrayed as graces with which God adorned ("garlanded") her; they seek to be clothed in grace and holiness like Mary, not so that they will attain her level of sanctity, but so that they might fulfill their Christian vocation of service, penance, and repentance for sins. It is interesting that, for all the high praise of Mary's perfection, she is nevertheless used as a model for Christians to hope to imitate; imitation of Mary, however, is not framed as an impossible aspiration to Mary's sinless nature, but a more

---

33. Burkhart, *Before Guadalupe*, 127.
34. Ibid., 129.

humble goal of analogous holiness and relationship with God, fit for those not uniquely chosen by God as Mary was. "You who are the leader, you who are the mirror, you who are the measuring stick . . . " proclaims Fray Juan Bautista, "May you . . . acknowledge us so that . . .we will be able to follow you through proper living, through good living, through pure being, through grace, so that . . . through you we will be favored."[35] Mary is conceived of here not as a distributor of graces, but as a guide for holy living.

DEVOTIONAL INCULTURATION: TRANSLATING MORE THAN WORDS ALONE

As noted above, the missionaries wasted no time in teaching the Nahua the basic prayers of the Christian tradition. Songs and pictorial representations aided their efforts, but no method could have been more effective than translating the prayers into the people's tongue, Nahuatl. Prayers translated into the vernacular in Europe, while sometimes suspect, were usually encouraged as a means of explaining the meaning of the prayers and encouraging their recitation, though it seems that the Latin was preferred by the clergy (for the sake of doctrinal purity) and the laity (for whom the Latin texts seemed superior in efficacy or authority). In New Spain, both Latin and vernacular (Nahuatl) versions of prayers were taught to and prayed by the native population, though Nahuatl seems to have been preferred. While the decrees of the Council of Trent on the topic of prayer severely limited the use of the vernacular in religious literature and prayer texts,[36] such regulations were slow to reach New Spain and slower to be enforced.[37] As we will see, the translation process is not purely linguistic—entire theological concepts and religious practices had to be translated and reimagined into the Nahuatl context. The extant translations of the *Ave Maria* into Nahuatl, for example, provide a fascinating window into the work of translating devotion—titles and salutations as well as piety and practice.

As seen in Sahagún's discourse on the *Ave Maria*, in his *Psalmodia Christiana* and in Fray Pedro de Gante's translation of the *Ave*, the Nahuatl translation of the ancient prayer from Latin conveys the sentiments of greeting, praise, and supplication in a manner different from the English translation. What in English is read as "Hail Mary" is expanded upon in

---

35. Ibid., 128.
36. Ibid., 3.
37. See Lara, "Roman Catholics in Hispanic America," 643–45.

Nahuatl: "Lady, Saint Mary, I greet you. May you be happy,"[38] Sahagún writes, whereas de Gante renders the greeting as "May you be joyful, oh Saint Mary."[39] "Ave" in Latin is merely a term of greeting, so the Nahuatl translations of Sahagún and de Gante are somewhat perplexing; likewise, the Spanish version of the prayer reads "Dios te salve, María," which differs from the Latin and English, to be sure, but not to the extent of the Nahuatl. The text of the prayer, however, was not originally composed in Latin, the Roman Catholic Church's primary liturgical language, but in Greek, the original language of the New Testament; this section of the prayer is drawn from the beginning of Luke's Gospel and was, therefore, originally composed in Greek. Leonardo Boff explains the full meaning of Gabriel's greeting in this larger scriptural context:

> The Greek term for 'hail' used by Luke (1:28) is *chaire*. . . . There is a connotation of joy in the word *chaire*, because in Greek 'joy' is *chára*, which has the same root as *cháris*, 'grace.' Many exegetes regard the 'hail' spoken by the angel to Mary as a simple greeting, albeit obviously very deferential, given the exceptional character of the circumstances. Others think that it is not properly a greeting, but an imperative, an invitation to joy. The correct translation would then be: 'Rejoice, Mary!' This meaning derives from the context of the entire periscope of the annunciation, which is based on three Old Testament prophecies: Zephaniah, Joel, and Zechariah.[40]

Sahagún and de Gante almost certainly knew Greek and were therefore most likely familiar with the slightly different meaning of the Greek version of the prayer. It is likely here that they are drawing upon the fuller Greek version of the Angelic greeting, not just the Latin or even the Spanish versions of the text. Furthermore, this interpretive choice is best suited for a translation of the text into Nahautl: Nahuatl poetic tradition favors the flowery, the exuberant, and the elaborate in addressing important figures and in relating important, supernatural, and true events.[41]

The petitionary phrase *ora pro nobis* ("pray for us" in English) is likewise rendered into Nahuatl in a manner distinct from the English or even the Spanish translations. Unlike Gabriel's greeting to Mary, this section of

---

38. Sahagún, *Psalmodia Christiana*, 23.
39. Burkhart, *Before Guadalupe*, 117.
40. Boff, *Praying with Jesus and Mary*, 154–55.
41. León-Portilla, *Aztec Thought*, 77–79.

the *Ave Maria* does not draw from the Gospel text, but is actually a later addition to the prayer itself.[42] The Nahuatl phrasing, "speak for us," on the one hand, adequately describes what is literally meant by "pray for us," and yet it lacks the spiritual and liturgical sense conveyed by *ora pro nobis*. On the other hand, the Nahuatl wording takes on another meaning, one that is not suggested by the Latin but which is pervasive in the popular tradition of Marian devotion: Mary as patroness of the devotee in the heavenly company, even solicitor of divine favor in a celestial courtroom. Given the bureaucratic nature of Spanish rule, this analogy would have made sense to Nahua devotees. As Burkhart explains, "Mary's role as advocate, although it did not have a direct precedent in Nahua religion, did have parallels in colonial life. The verb phrase assigned to intercession was *tepan tlahtoa* 'to speak for someone' (literally 'to say things on someone'); someone who does this is a *tepan tlahtoh*. These terms were applied to the activities of lawyers."[43]

These are but two examples of the issues involved in translating Marian prayers into a new language. The more complicated work of translating Marian devotions into a new culture, as noted previously, involved careful pastoral work: introducing new concepts, encouraging cultural appropriation, and often curtailing overzealous and misinterpreted pious practices. It is, of course, virtually impossible for modern scholars to measure the extent to which Marian theology was properly understood by Nahua converts and Marian devotion authentically practiced. Some evidence of Nahua piety, nevertheless, survives and can shed light on just how successful the friars were, on the one hand, in reworking European devotions into native practices and, on the other, in transforming Mary from the ruthless *conquistadora* of the Nahua into their adoring and adored mother.

Native wills written in Nahuatl—which existed before the conquest and continued, albeit altered into conformity with Christianity afterwards—witness to a thorough process of Christianization and, moreover, a native form of Marian devotion. Mary appeared frequently in native wills; while devotees usually bequeathed their goods to loved ones, they professed that their very souls were the property of the Virgin Mary.[44] Burkhart notes that rosaries were often present in these wills as well, appearing as cherished

---

42. Graef, *Mary: A History*, 181.
43. Burkhart, *Before Guadalupe*, 115.
44. Terraciano, "Native Expressions of Piety," 127–30.

religious objects gifted from one generation to the next.[45] Evidence of native acceptance of (and perhaps even appropriation of) the rosary shows that the devotion spread in popularity quickly and widely; the linguistic record, for example, supports this idea.

> Nahuas called the beads *cuentaxtli*, from Spanish *cuentas*; the addition of the absolutive suffix *-tli* to the Spanish noun indicates that this was a very early borrowing, thoroughly assimilated into Nahuatl. They referred to the prayer and the string of rosary beads in Nahuatl as Mary's flower necklace or flower jewel (*oxochicozcatzin*) rather than chaplet (*icpac xochitl* 'on-top-of-her flowers'). They would bring their beads to the priests to be blessed . . . According to Mendieta, among the Nahuas anyone who did not carry a rosary, as well as scourge for self-flagellation, "does not seem a Christian." Writing in the 1570s, Fray Diego Valadés observes that native people coming to church for communion come with their rosaries in their hands.[46]

As limited as our perspective into sixteenth century Nahua religiosity is, it witnesses to the unmistakable fact that, through the work of the friars, large numbers of the Nahua embraced Marian devotion within only a few decades of the inauguration of the missionary effort.

THE FRUIT OF DEVOTIONAL INCULTURATION? GUADALUPAN CATECHESIS

Perhaps the shining example of the success of the efforts of the missionaries of New Spain to inculturate Marian devotion is the rise of devotion to Our Lady of Guadalupe, a cult focused on a Marian shrine at Tepeyac and based, according to tradition, upon the Marian visions and miracles of a Christian Nahua man named Juan Diego in 1531. The earliest extant accounts of the tale of Juan Diego and Guadalupe come from two priests' texts—one in Spanish and one in Nahuatl—which were not written until the 1640s. Nevertheless, references to locally popular native devotion to the shrine at Tepeyac and the Marian image of Guadalupe exist from as early as 1556 and 1576. In 1556 the Franciscan provincial, Francisco de Bustamante, preached a sermon on the feast of Mary's Nativity that gave the historical record perhaps its earliest mention of native devotion to a

---

45. Burkhart, *Before Guadalupe*, 122–23.
46. Ibid., 123.

native shrine to Guadalupe at Tepeyac. Interestingly, Bustamante unabashedly voices his disapproval of the growing Nahua devotion to Guadalupe of Tepeyac, refuting the positive statements that the Dominican Archbishop (Alonso de Montúfar) had made about the popular shrine. It seems that Montúfar, hoping to encourage native Marian devotion, praised the shrine of Guadalupe at Tepeyac, voiced his official approval of it, and repeated stories of miracles worked there; Bustamante, in contrast, feared what the effects of over-emphasis on Mary's power and unfulfilled miracle requests would have upon the native populations' fledgling Marian devotion, which was still marred by confusion over whether or not Mary was a goddess.[47]

By 1576 it seems that the Nahua shrine to Our Lady of Guadalupe at Tepeyac had only grown in popularity among the native population. In his *Historia general*, Bernardino de Sahagún railed against aspects of Guadalupan devotion at Tepeyac which he perceived to be idolatrous.[48] It is interesting to note how Bernardino de Sahagún, author of such beautiful Nahuatl-language prayers and songs as found in his *Psalmodia Christiana*, whose missionary work resulted in such striking examples of inculturated devotional material as evidenced in the beginning of this essay, would take such issue with native expressions of Marian devotion at Tepeyac. While Sahagún suspected that the Tepeyac shrine formerly housed a temple to Tonantzin, Burkhart refutes his arguments, painting what Sahagún witnessed to be not syncretic pseudo-Christian worship, but authentic native expression of Marian devotion, centered at the exclusively-Marian site of Tepeyac:

> Sahagun's native informants never mentioned a preconquest shrine at Tepeyac. The Indians were not perpetuating memories of pre-Columbian goddesses but were projecting elements of their Christian worship into their pre-Christian past, conceptualizing their ancient worship in terms of Mary . . . There is no evidence that Tepeycac held any special meaning for sixteenth-century Indians.[49]

The earliest example of pro-Guadalupan missionary material meant for Nahua audiences, then, is the *Nican mopohua*, a Nahuatl account of the appearance of Mary to the Nahua Juan Diego and the miracles which followed. While the *Nican mopohua* is believed by some scholars to date to the

---

47. Poole, *Our Lady of Guadalupe*, 58–61.
48. Ibid., 79.
49. Burkhart, "Cult of the Virgin of Guadalupe," 208. Cited in Poole, *Our Lady of Guadalupe*, 79.

sixteenth century, its first appearance in surviving documentation is in the 1649 pastoral manual *Huei tlamahuiçoltica*, written by Luis Laso de la Vega.[50]

The *Huei tlamahuiçoltica* as a whole is a rich witness to the ongoing catechetical efforts of the Spanish missionaries, especially concerning Marian devotion. As Timothy Matovina notes, Laso de la Vega makes clear the catechetical intent of his work in the preface.[51] In an introductory supplication to the Virgin Mary herself, Laso de la Vega explains his purpose in retelling "the very great miracle by which you have appeared to people and have given them your image which is here in your precious home in Tepeyacac," and he prays that "the humble commoners see here and find out in their language all the charitable acts you have performed on their behalf."[52] The *Nican mopohua*, the heart of the manual, recounts the events surrounding Guadalupe and Juan Diego at Tepeyac. But it is Laso de la Vega's pastoral framework, particularly his closing prayer to Guadalupe, that is of most interest to us. Likely based upon the *Salve Regina*,[53] the "Prayer to be Directed to the Heavenly Queen, Our Precious Mother Guadalupe,"[54] begins by situating Mary in relation to the Trinity as "the precious daughter of God the Father . . . the precious mother of God's precious child . . . the precious spouse of God the Holy Spirit."[55] It continues by recalling the story of the Guadalupan apparition, recounting the miracles attributed to Guadalupe, and then asking for Guadalupe's continued aid in all things spiritual and worldly. The prayer closes by drawing upon themes found in other popular prayers—the *Ave Maria* and *Pater Noster*—invoking Guadalupe's aid "at the time of our death" in order to "put to flight our foe, who leads us astray" so that, with her intercession, her petitioners' souls may return to their creator.[56] The content of this prayer is clearly a fusion of traditional European prayer and Nahua sensibilities, in the context of Guadalupan devotion, which was presumably intended for memorization and recitation by her devotees (if Laso de la Vega's priestly readers should teach the prayer to their Nahua flocks). In conclusion, Laso de la Vega's pastoral manual represents an attempt on the part of Spanish priests to encourage devotion

50. Matovina, "First Guadalupan Pastoral Manual," 161.
51. Ibid., 163.
52. Laso de la Vega, *Huei tlamahuiçoltica*, 55.
53. Matovina, "First Guadalupan Pastoral Manual," 162.
54. Laso de la Vega, *Huei tlamahuiçoltica*, 127.
55. Matovina, "First Guadalupan Pastoral Manual," 171.
56. Laso de la Vega, *Huei tlamahuiçoltica*, 127.

to Guadalupe while presenting it as within the tradition of mainline Marian devotion as well as promoting Guadalupan devotions which parallel European Marian devotions. The final prayer in Laso de la Vega's work is a synthesis of Nahua and Spanish piety, employing popular native themes and imagery to teach proper Marian devotion and impart an orthodox understanding of Guadalupe.[57]

CONCLUSION

The inculturation of Marian devotion in New Spain began with mere translation, but from translation flowed transformation of thought, prayer, and devotion. We have seen how, "[t]ranslated into Nahuatl in New Spain, European discourses are no longer European, and Mary is no longer the same Mary. What changes is not simply a matter of language, the inadvertent shifts and lapses that result from the lack of equivalence between Spanish and Nahuatl or Latin and Nahuatl."[58] What changes, rather, is the way in which Mary is spoken of, conceived of, and even related to; the Marian devotion of the Nahua people was accomplished only through the holistic translation—and, therefore, transformation—of European Marian devotion and even the very relationship between the Nahua and Mary. What is perhaps most remarkable about this ongoing missionary effort of transforming devotion is the extremes: that the Nahua, who, in their own minds had apparently been conquered by the Spanish *conquistadora* as much as they had by the Spanish conquistadors, would so fully come to embrace Mary as their mother and Marian devotion as their primary form of pious expression that they would give rise to the indigenous Marian devotion which would come to transform the New World.

It is not surprising that, with the account of Mary appearing to one of the Nahua themselves—not in the form of the Spaniard's conquering queen, but as the brown-skinned native of Tepeyac—that the Nahua were able to accept what the missionaries had been preaching for years: that Mary was the Mother of their Savior, Jesus Christ, yes, but also *their own* mother, who cared deeply for the souls and welfare of the native population. As recounted in the *Nican mopohua*, Mary, dressed in familiar Nahua dress, and yet clothed with the sun and stars as the friars had so often described her in Assumption sermons, did not appear at Tepeyac at the request of

---

57. Matovina, "First Guadalupan Pastoral Manual," 170.
58. Burkhart, *Before Guadalupe*, 5.

the Spaniards in order to throw dirt in the eyes of the native people, to cheat them into defeat, or trick them into subjugation. The tradition held that at Tepeyac Mary showed herself as the mother and special protectress of the Nahua as well as the evangelizer to the New World. This tradition reflected even as it advanced the Marian teaching and devotion that Spanish missionaries had fostered among the Nahuas since the first evangelizers arrived in Mexico.

BIBLIOGRAPHY

Anderson, Arthur J.O. "The 'San Bernadino' of Sahagún's *Psalmodia*." Indiana 9 (1984) 107–14.
Boff, Leonardo. *Praying with Jesus and Mary*. Maryknoll, NY: Orbis, 2005.
Brading, D. A. *Mexican Phoenix*. New York: Cambridge University Press, 2002.
Burkhart, Louise M. *Before Guadalupe: The Virgin Mary in Early Colonial Nahuatl Literature*. Albany, NY: Institute for Mesoamerican Studies, University at Albany, 2001.
de Sahagún, Bernardino. *Psalmodia Christiana (Christian Psalmody)*. Translated by Arthur J.O. Anderson. Salt Lake City: University of Utah Press, 1993.
Graef, Hilda. *Mary: A History of Doctrine and Devotion*. Notre Dame, IN: Ave Maria, 2009.
Kroger, Joseph and Patrizia Granziera. *Aztec Goddesses and Christian Madonnas: Images of the Divine Feminine in Mexico*. Burlington, VT: Ashgate, 2012.
Lara, Jaime. "Roman Catholics in Hispanic America." In *The Oxford History of Christian Worship*, edited by Geoffrey Wainwright and Karen B. Westerfield Tucker, 633–50. New York: Oxford University Press, 2006.
León-Portilla, Miguel. *Aztec Thought and Culture*. Translated by Jack Emory Davis. Norman: University of Oklahoma Press, 1963.
Matovina, Timothy. "The First Guadalupan Pastoral Manual: Luis Laso de la Vega's *Huei tlamahuiçoltica* (1649)." *Horizons: The Journal of the College Theology Society* 40 (2013) 159–77.
Poole, Stafford. *Our Lady of Guadalupe: The Origins and Sources of a Mexican National Symbol, 1531–1797*. Tucson: University of Arizona Press, 1995.
Sousa, Lisa, Stafford Poole, and James Lockhart, eds. and trans. *The Story of Guadalupe: Luis Laso de la Vega's* Huei tlamahuiçoltica *of 1649*. Stanford: Stanford University Press, 1998.
Tanner, Norman and Sethina Watson. "Least of the Laity: the minimum requirements for a medieval Christian." Journal of Medieval History 32, (2006) 395–423.
Taylor, William B. "The Virgin of Guadalupe in New Spain: An Inquiry into the Social History of Marian Devotion," *American Ethnologist* 14.1 (1987) 9–33.
Terraciano, Kevin. "Native Expressions of Piety in Mixtec Testaments." In *Dead Giveaways: Indigenous Testaments of Colonial Mesoamerica and the Andes*, edited by Susan Kellogg. Salt Lake City: University of Utah Press, 1998.
Trexler, Richard C. *Church and Community, 1200–1600: Studies in the History of Florence and New Spain*. Rome: Edizioni di storia e letteratura, 1987.

3

Our Lady of Guadalupe in Art, 1606–1688: Growing the Devotion

Kate Macan

IN 1637, THE ECCLESIASTICAL council of the cathedral of Mexico issued an edict aimed at controlling the elaboration of replicas of Our Lady of Guadalupe's image. Posted on the cathedral doors in Mexico City, this public document included the accurate measurements of the titular image. According to the edict, any artist who did not faithfully represent the Virgin in his work and comply with the measurements for the image would face sanctions and penalties. Additionally, the council planned to confiscate all images of "inferior quality" that were in circulation.[1] Images deemed to be inferior were those that were incomplete, with the Virgin painted with her head or feet missing.[2]

At the time of the edict, replicas of the titular image were widely available because desire for a personal copy of Our Lady of Guadalupe had increased among the populace of New Spain following her reported role in mitigating the floods that plagued Mexico City from 1629 to 1634.[3] The artists of the day recognized the economic opportunity present in the growing demand for reproductions of the Guadalupe image. Hence, for the Roman Catholic curia, the edict served a dual purpose: it helped preserve the purity of the growing Guadalupan cult and it also allowed for the church to stake its claim in this new market. The edict of 1637 reveals that Guadalupe

---

1. Peterson, "Reproducibility of the Sacred," 56.
2. Ibid.
3. Ibid.

had risen in fame and popularity to the degree that reproductions of her image had to be regulated, frauds extirpated.

As a result of this seventeenth-century edict, it is likely that at least some if not a majority of early replicas of the Guadalupe image were confiscated and subsequently destroyed. Yet, several images from this time period *did* survive. Using these known works of art as guides, one can make some observations about the trajectory of Guadalupan devotional development and deduce the origins of beliefs and practices that are still popular today.

Artwork from the seventeenth century is a principal medium (another being written texts) by which one can better understand the origins of Guadalupan devotion. The art from this century, relatively understudied, is of particular importance in investigations into Guadalupan devotion because, at the date of her purported apparitions (1531) and in the centuries following, New Spain was a semi-literate society. The native peoples, one of whom is the central protagonist in the apparition accounts, were neophytes to the Spanish tongue and hence, often ignorant of the language in both spoken and written form. Paintings, unlike written texts or spoken sermons, have the ability to speak to all peoples. The paintings could communicate sacred truths to the rich and learned Spaniard, as well as the enslaved Indian. When displayed in prominent places of gathering, such as a church, paintings speak to thousands.

In many societies around the world, art was employed to teach the Christian faith and to impart important doctrines of Christian belief. New Spain was no exception. Art served a catechetical purpose. Works of art could and did reach a wide audience and taught the newly colonized Indians the Christian story. As will be explained, the Guadalupan art in particular records a story already circulating and one of its primary aims is to communicate the message of Guadalupe and her role as intercessor to others.

In order to explore the growing popularity of the nascent Guadalupan cult in New Spain, this essay will reflect on some of the earliest known visual representations of Our Lady of Guadalupe and her apparitions to Juan Diego. The author will assess what these early images tell us about the development of the devotion, the rise of the Guadalupan cult and evangelization in New Spain during the seventeenth century. These images, like the accounts penned by Miguel Sánchez (1648) and Luis Laso de la Vega (1649), are by no means all encompassing; they do not offer the entire picture, nor can they reconcile once and for all the historicity debates that surround the titular image and its origins. However, critically evaluating these early paintings can help us to nuance our understanding of the development of Guadalupan devotion because "they reveal a subtext often not present in documents."[4] What did the earliest artwork seek to communicate about Guadalupe? In what ways did it influence development of devotion to Guadalupe? The objective of this exercise is to determine how the art of the seventeenth century both reflected and inspired devotional practices to and beliefs about Our Lady of Guadalupe.

This investigation will feature artwork from 1606, the date of the first known reproduction of the Guadalupe image, to 1688, when Jesuit priest Francisco de Florencia (1620–1695) hyperbolically pronounced that every church in Mexico had an altar dedicated to Guadalupe.[5] This paper seeks to evaluate these early artistic works, already appraised for their historical significance, with regard to the role they play in Guadalupan devotion. This essay will examine selected art in a thematic fashion, focusing on the following three devotional developments evinced by the Guadalupan art of this century: the divine origins of the image itself and the sacramental nature of the *tilma*, Guadalupe's association with miracles and Guadalupe's role as intercessor, and finally, Guadalupe and her apparitions to the Indian Juan Diego as part of the story of salvation history.

In the progression of this essay, the artwork will be conversant with the earliest written theological studies of Guadalupe, Miguel Sánchez's 1648 patristic treatise *Imagen de la Virgen María (Image of the Virgin Mary)*, and Luis Laso de la Vega's 1649 pastoral manual, *Huei tlamahuiçoltica (By a Great Miracle)*.[6] To conduct this investigation, the author will draw on

4. Peterson, "Canonizing a Cult," 129.
5. Peterson, "Reproducibility of the Sacred," 60.
6. Both texts have longer names. The work by Miguel Sánchez is titled *Imagen de la Virgen María, Madre de Dios de Guadalupe: Milagrosamente aparecida en la ciudad de México: Celebrada en su historia, con la profecía del capítulo doce del Apocalipsis* (Image of the Virgin Mary, Mother of God of Guadalupe: Miraculously Appeared in the City of Mexico: Celebrated in Her History, with the Prophecy of Chapter Twelve of the Apocalypse). His work was first published in Mexico City by the Viuda de Bernardo Calderón (the widow of Bernardo Calderón) in 1648. The pastoral manual by Luis Laso de la Vega is titled *Huei tlamahuiçoltica omonexiti ilhuicac tlatocaçihuapilli Santa Maria totlaçonantzin Guadalupe in nican huei altepenahuac Mexico itocayocan Tepeyacac* (By a Great Miracle Appeared the Heavenly Queen, Saint Mary, Our Precious Mother of Guadalupe, Here Near the Great Altepetl of Mexico, at a Place Called Tepeyac). His work was originally published in Mexico City by Imprenta de Juan Ruiz in 1649. It was reprinted with an English translation in *The Story of Guadalupe: Luis Laso de la Vega's Huei tlamahuiçoltica of 1649*, Sousa et al. Little is known about the life of Luis Laso de

the previous efforts of art historians—Jeanette Peterson, Jaime Cuadriello, Elisa Vargas Lugo and Clara Bargellini—to interpret and better understand early Guadalupan art. The scholarship of said art historians will provide the foundation for the connections the author intends to make.

DIVINE ORIGINS OF THE TITULAR IMAGE

The titular image, currently on display in the Basilica of Our Lady of Guadalupe in Mexico City, is popularly believed to be a miraculously produced portrait of the Virgin. In the earliest known piece of Guadalupan art, a reinterpretation of the Guadalupe image on the *tilma*, the Spanish artist Baltasar de Echave Orio (1548–1623) communicates this belief, transmitting the message of Guadalupe's divine authorship to the viewer. This replica, dated to 1606, is significant because it is "the oldest signed and dated copy known."[7] As such, this image offers insight into the early stages of Guadalupan devotion, indicating that by this point in time some devotees were venerating her image and the *tilma*.

The work itself is "a unique and remarkably faithful copy of the sixteenth-century *tilma* icon."[8] Echave Orio's emphasis on the sacred nature of the cloth is a distinctive feature of this painting. In the piece, Echave Orio, at the time the most famous artist in New Spain, diligently replicates both the image of the Virgin and the *tilma* and creates a "tangibly real and . . . permanent relic."[9] His painting is a representation of the entire cloak of Juan Diego. Not only does he faithfully represent the cloak, but Echave Orio also fabricated "his work out of two similarly joined vertical canvas strips to simulate the sewn panels of the tilma . . . ."[10]

This painting is noteworthy for two reasons. First, this image indicates that by this point in time Our Lady of Guadalupe already had patrons. In the seventeenth century, any artwork of size and caliber, such as this 1606 work, was commissioned. An average person would not have had the means

---

la Vega. The dates of his birth and death are unknown. Scholars estimate that Miguel Sánchez was born in 1594 in Mexico City. He was a priest and well trained in the works of St. Augustine as well as dedicated to Our Lady of Guadalupe. A *criollo* by birth, Sánchez died in his native land in 1674.

7. Chávez, *Our Lady of Guadalupe*, 51.
8. Peterson, "Canonizing a Cult," 129.
9. Ibid.
10. Ibid.

and/or skills to produce grand works of art. Thus, at least some people, including persons of significance, had heard of Our Lady of Guadalupe and felt it appropriate to venerate her image through a faithful reproduction.

Secondly, this piece is significant because of Echave Orio's focus on the *tilma*. Peterson writes, "this work makes a claim for the inherent mediating power of the sacred cloth itself."[11] This idea, that the cloth itself has sacred powers, is similar to beliefs about the sudarium, Veronica's veil.[12] The artistic gesture of replicating the *tilma* is not trivial. It signals that Echave Orio and/or his patron(s) believed the image was not painted by human hands or, at minimum, they believed that the *tilma* had miraculous powers.[13] This piece of art indicates that by 1606 the *tilma* itself was already part of the devotion. People in New Spain believed it was miraculous. While this evidence does not prove that the story of Guadalupe's apparitions to Juan Diego existed at this time, it does suggest the idea that "oral versions . . . may have well been circulating."[14] Including the tilma in the reproduction provides evidence that at the dawn of the seventeenth century some people in New Spain believed the *tilma* had divine or miraculous origins.

In his book, Sánchez also comments on the miraculous origins of the image on the *tilma*. He includes a lengthy section on what believers see when they gaze on Guadalupe's image.[15] In this section of the book, he declares that Guadalupe is "the unique, singular, only, and rare" image of the Virgin Mary "in all of Christendom painted with flowers."[16] Sánchez commits to paper a belief about the image that was enshrined by Echave Orio in his painting years earlier: the image itself was not made by human hands. As will be detailed in a later section, this association between Guadalupe and the miraculous becomes even more prominent in seventeenth-century artwork following the publication of Sánchez's treatise.

11. Ibid., 130.

12. It is believed that the image on Veronica's veil, that of Christ's face, was made when she wiped the face of Jesus in route to his crucifixion. This icon, like the one on Juan Diego's *tilma*, is "thought to have been made by contact with the original sacred personage." Bargellini, "Originality and Invention," 85.

13. Peterson, "Canonizing a Cult," 130. Peterson presents a more detailed discussion of Echave Orio's work and its significance in *Visualizing Guadalupe: From Black Madonna to Queen of the Americas*. See specifically p. 159.

14. Ibid.

15. Matovina, "Guadalupe at Calvary," 804. For Sánchez's full discussion, see *Imagen de la Virgen*, 198–236.

16. Sánchez, *Imagen de la Virgen*, 206. The translation is mine.

In *Imagen de la Virgen María*, Sánchez includes the story of the apparitions of Our Lady of Guadalupe to Juan Diego at Tepeyac. Luis Laso de la Vega does the same in his publication the following year. In the narrative, the Virgin visits Juan Diego at Tepeyac and asks him to petition the bishop to build her a temple. After a failed attempt to present her petition before then bishop of Mexico City, Juan de Zumárraga, Juan Diego asks the Virgin for a sign to take to the bishop. The bishop, doubtful of the Indian's story, requests proof from Juan Diego before he will agree to build a church for the Virgin at Tepeyac. As testimony of her appearance, the Virgin offers Juan Diego out-of-season flowers; but she not only offers flowers, as an image of the Virgin is revealed when Juan Diego unveils his *tilma* in front of the bishop and his servants. In the apparition accounts by Sánchez and Laso de la Vega, flowers become the medium by which the miraculous image was imprinted on the *tilma*.

Following the publication of *Imagen de la Virgen María* and *Huei tlamahuiçoltica*, flowers are consistently present in artistic renditions of the apparition scenes. They become "both the medium and the agent of the miraculous image."[17] In the latter half of the seventeenth century, "references to the passing of the roses from Juan Diego to the Virgin and back again into the cloth" became commonplace.[18] Notably, a 1667 piece by Juan Correa (Fig. I) focuses on the sacramental nature of the flowers, as, "the roses were, after all, the instrument of contact between Mary and the cloth."[19]

Several years later, in 1670, Juan Sánchez Salmerón painted a canvas with the figure of the Holy Spirit painting Our Lady of Guadalupe.[20] In this piece, "the canvas shows a heavenly atelier in which the Holy Spirit is painting the Virgin while God the Father and Son hold the canvas and angels serve as assistants."[21] This painting echoes the belief that the image was not of human hands, but rather divine work. Additionally, the archangels Gabriel and Michael appear in the scene, inviting the viewer to recall the Annunciation and the Woman of the Apocalypse in Revelation 12.

As Correa and Salmerón's efforts indicate, throughout the course of the century, artists remained attentive to communicating the divine origins of the image on the *tilma*. An anonymous engraving, later attributed to

---

17. Peterson, "Reproducibility of the Sacred," 67.
18. Bargellini, "Originality and Invention," 86.
19. Ibid.
20. The dates of Sánchez Salmerón's birth and death are unknown.
21. Bargellini, "Originality and Invention," 88.

our lady of guadalupe in art, 1606–1688

Antonio Castro and included in an early edition of the work *La Felicidad de Mexico* by Luis Becerra Tanco (1675) also had such aims.[22] In the engraving, Castro sought to explain scientifically how the image of the Virgin came to be imprinted on Juan Diego's cloak. The engraving suggests that the sun—divine light—imprinted the image on the *tilma*.

The divine origins of the image received particular attention in 1666 when the first official examination of *tilma* image took place. The examination occurred as a stage in the capitular inquiry of 1665–1666 into the Guadalupan tradition and the miraculous appearance of the image on the tilma. This inquiry was part of an effort to petition the pope to make December 12 (the reported date of Guadalupe's appearance on the *tilma*) a feast day in all of New Spain and an attempt to gain papal approval for the account of the apparitions.[23] In addition to assessing the image, "testimonials to the apparition were taken from local Indians," as part of the official Church authentication.[24] The inquiry was aimed at establishing a continuity of tradition.[25]

Painters of the day participated as part of a special committee to investigate the image. The painters who examined the *tilma* "declared the image miraculous and perfect. They adduced as proof the technical impossibility of painting directly on such a rough surface."[26] The committee accordingly concluded that only God could be responsible for such work. Likewise, a second group that examined the image a few weeks later determined that for the image to maintain its brilliance in such a humid climate was a miracle in and of itself.[27]

Growing demand to have a "true copy" of Our Lady of Guadalupe, coupled with the work of Echave Orio and his successors, provides evidence that the populace in New Spain maintained belief that the *tilma* had both miraculous origins and powers. This belief inspired the common practice among artists to certify that their works had touched the *tilma* image. The works, it was believed, by virtue of touch, inherited the supernatural power of the titular image.

---

22. For a visual of this image, see Vargas Lugo, "Iconología Guadalupana," 74.
23. Poole, *Our Lady of Guadalupe*, 128.
24. Taylor, "Virgin of Guadalupe," 15.
25. Poole, *Our Lady of Guadalupe*, 138.
26. Bargellini, "Originality and Invention," 88.
27. Poole, *Our Lady of Guadalupe*, 142

As replicas of the image of Guadalupe on the *tilma* and interpretations of the apparition scenes grew in number, the most "authentic" renditions were those that had come in physical contact with the titular image. Artists of the day certified their reproductions with inscriptions at the bottom of their works and "such inscribing was particularly done if the copies touched by the original were destined for transoceanic export."[28] Such reproductions testify that the painting by Echave Orio initiated a trend in Guadalupan art, promoting a belief in the image's divine origin.

The credence in the transferability of the miraculous powers of the *tilma* is explicit in a 1656 work by José Juárez (1617–1661). Juárez, a Creole artist, painted the *Virgin of Guadalupe with Apparitions* for a Conceptionist convent in Spain. The abbess of the convent, Sr. Maria de Agreada, commissioned the work. Juárez labeled the painting "a 'true portrait and exact copy' and indicates that his painting was 'touched to the original.'"[29]

ASSOCIATION WITH MIRACLES

As devotion to Guadalupe grew, so too did belief in her role as intercessor. A second thread apparent in early Guadalupan art is Guadalupe's association with miracles. She became, in Peterson's words, a "wonder-working Virgin."[30] The earliest piece from this period that communicates Guadalupe's connection with miracles is a work known as the Stradanus engraving (1613).[31] The engraving (Fig. II) is the second-earliest known reproduction of the Virgin of Guadalupe and it predates Sánchez's account by more than 30 years. The engraving was crafted by Samuel Stradanus, a Flemish artist, and commissioned by Archbishop Juan Pérez de la Serna.[32] The image was elaborated in an effort to help raise funds to build a proper basilica at Tepeyac, the site of the Guadalupan shrine. As inscribed on the

---

28. Cuadriello, Introduction to *La Reina de las Américas*, 11.
29. Bargellini, "Originality and Invention," 87.
30. Peterson, "Canonizing a Cult."
31. Though other scholars date the engraving to somewhere between 1615 and 1622, Peterson, in a recent book chapter, "Canonizing a Cult: A Wonder-Working Guadalupe in the Seventeenth Century," dates the engraving to 1613. For a full explanation of her reasoning, see page 131.
32. There is little information available about Stradanus's life. We do know that he was active in New Spain from 1604–1626.

plate, in exchange for a donation to help support the building of the church, the donor would receive forty days of indulgence.

The archbishop commissioned Stradanus to develop "an appropriate fundraising tool with accessible visual appeal."[33] Thus, Stradanus worked to create a copper plate that could be used to produce broadsheets of the engraving. Based on the condition of the plate, it is clear that a multitude of sheets were printed; it is so worn that some of the details of the image are "almost unintelligible."[34]

The Stradanus image provides evidence that the devotion was expanding in the early seventeenth century. Since it could be easily reproduced, the Stradanus image also suggests that knowledge of the Guadalupan cult extended beyond the geographical area around Tepeyac to Mexico City and the environs. However, it is difficult to determine just how widely the copies of the engraving circulated.

For the purposes of this study, this work is of import because of the way it aims to develop devotion to Our Lady of Guadalupe. The Stradanus piece suggests that from early on devotees associated Guadalupe with miracles. In the images included in the Stradanus engraving, there is a heavy focus on the Virgin's accessibility and efficacy in moments of illness or suffering. In the Stradanus piece, all those pictured in the miracle stories receive Guadalupe's help; illnesses are cured and traumatic effects of accidents reversed. The engraving is aimed at communicating to viewers that miracles await those who seek out the Virgin and venerate her. For example, in the vignettes, Guadalupe cures the son of the sacristan of the hermitage at Tepeyac, Juan Pavón; she cures a Discalced Franciscan, Pedro de Valderrama, who was troubled by a tumorous toe; Bartholomé Grandía, a Spaniard, is cured of his headaches; and she saves Antonio de Carvajal's son during a horse riding accident.[35]

Peterson classifies the engraving as a type of "'graphic sermon.'"[36] This style of engraving, she writes, was popular at the time in Spain and other European countries. As such, its transferal to New Spain is not surprising. Peterson claims that such images were used to teach "doctrinal, biblical and moral lessons by illustrating the model of a virtuous, often sacrificial life," and they feature hagiographic stories that call attention to the saint's ability

33. Peterson, "Canonizing a Cult," 131.
34. Ibid.
35. Poole, *Our Lady of Guadalupe*, 123–24.
36. Peterson, "Canonizing a Cult," 133.

to heal and protect the devotee in times of trouble.[37] In bringing their needs to the Virgin, the inhabitants of New Spain would thus also be acting virtuously, trusting her with their trials and cares. The design of the Stradanus image, mimicking the dynamic of the graphic sermon, makes it clear that a relationship with the Virgin of Guadalupe would secure her protection for the believer.

It must be noted that the Stradanus engraving's primary purpose was to raise funds for the building of a new church; however, a secondary and indirect motive behind the elaboration of the engraving was the promotion of pilgrimages to the site of Tepeyac so believers could experience the presence and protection of Our Lady of Guadalupe. Like the persons imaged in the side panels of the engraving, those viewing the image would receive divine healing if they too visited Tepeyac. As theologian Timothy Matovina writes, the Stradanus engraving reveals that " . . . blessings and miracles await those who appeal to Guadalupe and contemplate her countenance and holy image."[38] The viewer was encouraged to pray to the Virgin in illness or tragedy because she would intercede with God on his/her behalf. Like the titular image itself, the Stradanus image portrays the Virgin in a prayer posture. Adherence to this posture is significant because "Prayer was the instrument both of Mary's intercession with God and of the believer's appeal to her."[39]

The Virgin occupies the central frame of the engraving and is surrounded by eight lateral panels that offer testimony in word and image of her efficacy as intercessor. The eight miracle scenes in the Stradanus image are "apparently drawn from ex-votos . . . supplicants had enshrined at the Guadalupe chapel."[40] Ex-votos are testimonials in word and image of the Virgin's powers. Stradanus became aware of the miracles either through his own visits to the shrine or through popular narratives (oral or written) that were based on the miracle accounts. This engraving is of consequence because it indicates that by the date of its production in 1613, eight miracle stories, and perhaps more, associated with Guadalupe were known.[41]

---

37. Ibid.
38. Matovina, "Theologies of Guadalupe," 71.
39. Taylor, "Virgin of Guadalupe," 20.
40. Matovina, "First Guadalupan Pastoral Manual," 165.
41. Poole, *Our Lady of Guadalupe*, 124.

In the Stradanus engraving the principal image of the Virgin is that of "a robust Flemish matron."[42] In fact, she only mildly resembles the image of the Virgin on the *tilma*. Peterson writes, "the engraved Virgin is animated by a beatific smile and dynamic sway of her pose."[43] As evidenced by this interpretation of Our Lady of Guadalupe, "reproductions of the Virgin were not yet codified nor dependent on the painstaking tracings derived from a template" which later became common practice.[44]

The Virgin appears in a liturgical setting, flanked by candles and hovering above the altar in a prayer pose. In the main image, and in all appearances of the Virgin in the vignettes, she is "treated as a free floating vision" and the *tilma* is not present.[45] Beatriz Berndt León Mariscal speculates the *tilma* is absent in an effort to emphasize her celestial nature.[46] Peterson says, "the miraculous powers attributed to Guadalupe are channeled through the Virgin's presence in the lives of New Spain's inhabitants and through the implicit sacrality of her shrine-home . . . ."[47] Thus, using the Stradanus image as a gauge, one can conclude that at least by this date, Guadalupe's image was on display at her hermitage at Tepeyac.[48]

As this paper does not permit an in-depth analysis of all eight lateral panels of the Stradanus image, we will focus our attention on one in particular. Worthy of mention is the second panel (Fig. III). A nun, Catharina de Niehta, drinks from a spring and is cured from the dropsy that had plagued her for eleven years.[49] The image "states that Catharina drinks water from the fountain 'where Guadalupe appeared' and then she was cured."[50] The image coupled with the text *does* affirm that an apparition happened, however it is ambiguous whether the apparition mentioned is in reference to the Virgin's apparitions to Juan Diego or whether it references an apparition in connection with Catharina's healing.[51] If the scene indeed intends to

42. Peterson, "Canonizing a Cult," 134.

43. Ibid.

44. Ibid., 134–35.

45. Ibid., 133.

46. León Mariscal, "Miracles," 107.

47. Peterson, "Canonizing a Cult," 133.

48. An engraving that appears in Sánchez's book also features the Virgin in a liturgical setting. This engraving provides additional evidence that the Guadalupe image was on display for veneration at Tepeyac prior to 1648.

49. Peterson, "Canonizing a Cult," 145–46.

50. Ibid., 148.

51. Ibid.

highlight the former, then one can affirm that devotees were aware of the Virgin's apparitions to Juan Diego before 1613, indicating the tradition was well beyond its beginning phases. However, arriving at such a conclusion is presently challenging due to the current lacuna of evidence. Nonetheless, this image is significant because it communicates Guadalupe's active presence in the lives of her devotees and her care for their well-being.

Peterson, in her most recent book, *Visualizing Guadalupe: From Black Madonna to Queen of the Americas*, concludes:

> ... the [Stradanus] broadsheet is not entirely a top-down manifestation, nor were the miracles invented wholesale. They represent official recognition of popular beliefs, thus ensuring a positive reception. The Echave Orio 1606 painting is similarly a Church-sponsored and -sanctioned effort to promulgate the cult, but also reflects entrenched beliefs.[52]

The thematic present in the Stradanus engraving is also found in the books by Sánchez and Laso de la Vega. Much like in the Stradanus work, the two authors included miracle accounts to attest to Guadalupe's power, attract devotees to the shrine, and in Laso de la Vega's case, to provide sermon illustrations for preachers. There is a discrepancy in the content and number of miracles featured in the Stradanus engraving and in the works by Sánchez and Laso de la Vega, though also considerable overlap in the miraculous incidents that each source recounts. This leads some, such as historian Stafford Poole, to speculate that Sánchez and Laso de la Vega had access to an earlier written anthology of miracles unknown to Stradanus, or that they worked with stories popular in oral tradition.[53] In his work, Laso de la Vega includes an undated collection of miracle stories known as the *Nican motecpana*. It is hypothesized that the work is "a compilation of miracle stories associated with the shrine but with diverse origins."[54] There is a lively debate among scholars as to its authorship and when the text was written, specifically as to whether it pre-dates the Stradanus engraving. However, regardless whether an earlier written work existed, with the Stradanus image we do know that by 1613 there are visual claims for Guadalupe's ability to intervene on behalf of her faithful.

---

52. Peterson, *Visualizing Guadalupe*, 158.
53. Poole, *Our Lady of Guadalupe*, 119.
54. Ibid.

our lady of guadalupe in art, 1606–1688

Both Sánchez and Laso de la Vega recount the moment when Our Lady of Guadalupe performed her first favor for a native of the Americas.[55] This miracle is imaged in an anonymous mid-seventeenth century work, *El Primer Milagro* (The First Miracle), which Peterson attributes to the workshop of José Juárez. According to the miracle account, after Guadalupe's image had been revealed to Bishop Juan de Zumárraga, it was carried in a procession from Mexico City to Tepeyac as "part of the celebration of the dedication of the first ermita . . . on 26 December 1531."[56] During a mock skirmish in the procession, a stray arrow struck and killed an indigenous participant.[57] The native was placed before the image of Our Lady of Guadalupe and was revived, his wound cured.

This painting, *El Primer Milagro* (1653), is noteworthy for its size.[58] Jaime Cuadriello calls the painting a "testimonial image."[59] Cuadriello says that the image is both "narratively and ethnographically accurate," as it depicts Spaniards and natives in the procession.[60] Also of note is that this miracle account reflects the idea of the Virgin's special care for the Indians. The painting, much like the Stradanus engraving, is aimed at visually recounting the miracle story and communicating to the viewer Guadalupe's efficacy in healing miracles. Peterson notes that the painting likely reached a wide and diverse audience, as it was hung in "her sanctuary's presbytery in Mexico City."[61]

A final image worthy of mention is an anonymous work dated to the 17th century titled *La Virgen de Guadalupe intercede por la salvación de un alma y Cristo la redime* (Virgin of Guadalupe intercedes for the salvation of a soul and Christ redeems him). In this painting more so than the others considered thus far, the role and power of Guadalupe as intercessor is apparent. The Virgin, imaged as Guadalupe, lovingly looks on as the crucified Christ reaches down from the cross to embrace a soul caught betwixt heaven and hell, symbolized by an angel and devil respectively. The Virgin's eyes are fixed upon the soul, whose facial expression is one of terror and fright. Her expression and countenance are calm, evincing an aura of peace.

55. Ibid. This miracle account is not included in the Stradanus engraving.
56. Ibid.
57. Ibid.
58. The painting is approximately nine feet by twenty feet.
59. Cuadriello, Introduction to *La Reina de las Américas*, 14.
60. Ibid.
61. Peterson, *Visualizing Guadalupe*, 203.

This image testifies to the ultimate power of Guadalupe; she is an efficacious, accessible, "wonder-working" Virgin capable of persuading her son to grant salvation to sinners.

This image alludes to another element in the development of Guadalupan devotion. As implied by this work, Guadalupe functioned as a corrective to an authoritarian Christ. Guadalupe countered a prevailing belief in sixteenth and seventeenth century Catholicism in a dominant and stern father God.[62] Images like this anonymous work teach the faithful to approach the Virgin of Guadalupe with their needs and concerns because she will present those needs before God. Painted as approachable and sympathetic, she functions as a foil to a punishing and stern father God and she is capable of working miracles for her faithful, as she did for those imaged in the Stradanus engraving.

GUADALUPE EVENT AS PART OF SALVATION HISTORY

Based on the artistic evidence presented, one can assert that both Sánchez and Laso de la Vega were part of an evolving campaign that started in the late sixteenth or early seventeenth century to enshrine the Virgin of Guadalupe as one of the prominent images of Mary in New Spain. As the cult of Guadalupe grew, believers sought to explain her unique role in salvation history. Unlike another miraculous image of the Virgin, Guadalupe of Extremadura, Guadalupan devotees came to conclude that she was not crafted by St. Luke or miraculously found.[63] Christians in New Spain came to consider this image of the Virgin Mary unique because they believed it was not made by human hands, and devotees reverenced this image of the Blessed Mother because they believed the image to be the Virgin herself.

In textual form, Miguel Sánchez was the first to take up the task of reading the image of Guadalupe through the lens of salvation history.

---

62. This idea is presented in a book chapter by Louise Burkhart titled "'Here is Another Marvel': Marian Miracle Narratives in a Nahuatl Manuscript." In the chapter, Burkhart details how in the early Nahuatl miracle narratives Mary was imaged as more approachable, a foil to a distant and stern God.

63. Another popular image of the Virgin in New Spain during this time period was the Spanish Virgin of Guadalupe, Guadalupe de Extremadura, a European black Madonna. Her devotees believed St. Luke carved the statue. The sculpture was reportedly hidden for a time in the mountains of Extremadura during the Moorish occupation of Spain. At the beginning of the fourteenth century, the Virgin appeared to a humble shepherd and he discovered the sculpture, over 600 years later.

Sánchez examines "Guadalupe and the evangelization of Mexico vis-à-vis the wider Christian tradition."[64] In his patristic treatise, Sánchez concludes that the image of the Virgin on the *tilma* is the Woman of the Apocalypse (Rev 12). For Sánchez, the biblical text "Revelation 12 prefigured Mexico, Guadalupe, and the destiny of the sons of the land,"[65] and, ". . . the woman in Revelation 12 is identified with the Church and Mary and, by extension, with Guadalupe."[66] Sánchez attempts to use biblical narratives to interpret and understand the current events of his day. He includes biblical images commonly associated with Mary in his work: Jacob's ladder, the Burning Bush, the Rose of Jericho.[67] Written for the learned class, Sánchez's work provides a new lens by which to view and understand the image. Subsequently, seventeenth-century artists (and their patrons) also started to use this lens to image Guadalupe and transmit her story.

Just as artists were important to the spread of the idea of the divine origin of the image and the miracle accounts, they were likewise influential in spreading the story of the Virgin's apparitions to Juan Diego at Tepeyac as another chapter in the story of salvation history. The artists of the time period incorporated Sánchez's theological analysis and typological reading of the image into their works. Most Spaniards, *criollos*, and natives in New Spain likely first learned about Guadalupe's appearances to Juan Diego through art and via sermons.

The Virgin of Guadalupe, according to Sánchez, was the same woman, "clothed with the sun," who appeared to St. John on the island of Patmos (Rev 12:1). A seventeenth-century painting, attributed to Juan Correa, images this scene along with Guadalupe's apparitions to Juan Diego at Tepeyac. The titular image of Our Lady of Guadalupe is the central image on this canvas. Surrounding this image, the artist depicts the apparition scenes as described by Sánchez and Laso de la Vega.[68] Below Guadalupe's feet, one finds a vignette of her appearance to St. John, writing Revelation, at Patmos. The image of the Virgin in the scene with St. John is the same as the

64. Matovina, "Theologies of Guadalupe," 66.
65. Poole, *Our Lady of Guadalupe*, 107.
66. Matovina, "Guadalupe at Calvary," 801.
67. Sánchez, *Imagen de la Virgen*, 214.
68. There is a discrepancy between the number of apparitions included in each account. There are five apparitions in the account by Sánchez and only four in the *Nican mopohua*, Laso de la Vega's work. The *Nican mopohua* does not include the third apparition from Sánchez's work. In this apparition, Juan Diego tells the Virgin about his interview with the bishop. For further detail, see Poole, *Our Lady of Guadalupe*, 112.

image displayed in the center of the work and in the apparition scenes with Juan Diego. The fact that these images of Guadalupe are identical serves to link the events: her appearance to St. John at Patmos and her appearance to Juan Diego at Tepeyac.

Moreover, it is notable that at the top of the canvas there is a white bird sustaining the central image of the Virgin. Art historians are undecided as to whether the bird is meant to represent the Holy Spirit or the Mexican eagle.[69] The archangels Gabriel and Michael flank Guadalupe on both sides. By including the angels Gabriel and Michael, Correa also signals that this image of the Virgin Mary, Our Lady of Guadalupe, is the Virgin of the Annunciation and the woman of Revelation 12.[70]

Finally, this painting is significant because rose blossoms appear throughout the canvas, in the spaces between the different apparition scenes. These blossoms are the "artistic summation of the words with which Miguel Sánchez prefaced his book (And there appeared a great wonder in Heaven) through which three annunciations were linked to the work of salvation."[71] Cuadriello writes that traditionally, the first two annunciations are considered to be the appearance of the Holy Spirit to Mary in Nazareth, heralded by the Archangel Gabriel, and Mary's apparition to St. John in Patmos, which is validated by the Archangel Michael. The appearance of the Virgin to Juan Diego (and by extension to the Mexican church) is logically the third annunciation in Cuadriello's estimation.[72] Identifying Guadalupe's apparition to Juan Diego as an annunciation speaks to the importance of the event not only for the people of New Spain, but for believers elsewhere as well—the Tepeyac event is part of salvation history.

A second work from the seventeenth century that is emblematic of how artists interpreted the image of Our Lady of Guadalupe vis-à-vis the wider Christian tradition is an anonymous work titled *Virgen de Guadalupe coronada por la santísma Trinidad* (Virgin of Guadalupe Crowned by the Holy Trinity). On this canvas, the titular image of the Virgin is surrounded by the five apparition scenes, including her appearance to and healing of

---

69. For example, Vargas Lugo, in "Iconología Guadalupana" (90), says that the bird is the Mexican eagle. Cuadriello, in "Visions from Patmos-Tenochtitlan" (67), claims that the bird is the Holy Spirit.

70. In Luke's Gospel, the angel Gabriel visits Mary in Nazareth to announce the birth of Jesus (1:26–38). The angel Michael appears in Rev 12:7–8.

71. Cuadriello, "Visions from Patmos-Tenochtitlan," 68.

72. Ibid.

our lady of guadalupe in art, 1606–1688

Juan Diego's uncle, Juan Bernardino.[73] Additionally, images of well-known biblical scenes are included on the canvas: Jacob's ladder, St. John writing the book of Revelation, an image of the celestial Jerusalem. At the cusp of the canvas is an image of the Holy Trinity.[74] The placement of this imagery referencing biblical events and dogmatic truths next to Our Lady of Guadalupe allows for the viewer to make the connection that the Guadalupe event was both providential for and exclusive to the inhabitants of New Spain.[75] Intentionally or not, this artist has translated ideas presented in Sánchez's text into visual form.[76]

As already alluded to, it is hard to determine exactly when the earliest visual reinterpretations of the apparition accounts were created. Yet, as artists continued to interpret the image of Our Lady of Guadalupe and the apparition accounts, they had license to emphasize the elements of the story they and their patrons deemed most important. For example, this interpretive license is evident in a sketch of the fourth apparition included in Sánchez's work. In the sketch, Juan Diego unveils his *tilma* before the bishop, revealing the image of Our Lady of Guadalupe. This sketch in Sánchez's work highlights Juan Diego's transformation from an Indian, who was viewed as inferior, to Our Lady of Guadalupe's chosen messenger. The anonymous artist images Juan Diego as taller and more important than Bishop Zumárraga. He is standing and the bishop is kneeling. This image, and others like it, announce to the population of New Spain Guadalupe's ability to transform and humanize. This scene, which becomes prominent in later works, serves "as a symbolic testimony that the Indian, as much as the Spaniard, was capable of being saved, capable of receiving Christianity."[77]

Later in the century, the unveiling of Guadalupe on the *tilma* became the principal image in Guadalupan art. In many instances, it replaced the titular image of Guadalupe herself. This dynamic is seen in a piece by Juan Correa (1667). In Correa's image, the Virgin is not central; rather, the most important visual on the canvas is Juan Diego opening his *tilma* before Bishop Zumárraga.

---

73. Of the apparition scenes imaged in the seventeenth century, this scene is the one least frequently imaged. Based upon the artist's inclusion of five apparitions, it is possible to speculate that he was working with ideas from Sánchez's text, as Laso de la Vega only includes four apparitions.

74. Vargas Lugo, "Iconología Guadalupana," 90.

75. Ibid.

76. These ideas appear in Sánchez, *Imagen de la Virgen*, 214

77. Wolf, "Virgin of Guadalupe," 37.

As miracle stories about Guadalupe, such as those imaged in the Stradanus engraving, were propagated and the works by Sánchez and Laso de la Vega read and shared, demand for copies of Guadalupe extended beyond the bounds of New Spain. By the mid-seventeenth century, if not before, Our Lady of Guadalupe had international devotees. The 1656 work by José Juárez was destined for a Conceptionist monastery in Spain, for example.

In the painting, Juárez omits key scenes from Sánchez's work. Since Juárez is one of the first artists to paint the apparition scenes collectively, he does not image Juan Diego telling the Virgin about his unsuccessful meeting with the bishop, nor does he include the scene where Juan Diego tries to avoid the Virgin in an effort to seek medical care for his sick uncle.[78] Instead of including these scenes, which later become conventional in Guadalupan art, Juárez focuses on Juan Diego asking the Virgin for a sign to convince the bishop of her apparitions and on the miraculous blossoming of out-of-season flowers on the hill of Tepeyac.

Underneath the apparition scenes, Juárez includes captions to explain to the viewer what is happening in each vignette. These captions are relevant because they indicate that at the time Juárez was painting, the apparition stories were not yet well known, despite the fact that, as mentioned above, there were international devotees. By including captions in his piece destined for the Spanish monastery, Juárez hopes "to explain a narrative not yet familiar to a broad audience."[79] In many senses of the word, Juárez is setting forth standards for what would become tradition by the end of the century. In later pieces that feature the apparition scenes at Tepeyac, captions are not present—artists presume that the viewers already know the story.

In this mid-century piece, the artist gives great physical presence to Juan Diego.[80] He is attentive to the demeanor of the native and in the apparition scenes Juan Diego displays life-like gestures.[81]

Juárez's piece is also striking for how it communicates the type of relationship that existed between Juan Diego and the Virgin. In the ways the two figures on the canvas are animated, it is clear that they have a relationship of intimacy.[82] According to Peterson, ". . . in the scenes leading to the final

---

78. These are the second and the fourth apparitions in the Sánchez account. The apparition scene where Juan Diego tells the Virgin about his interview with the bishop is absent in the *Nican mopohua*.

79. Peterson, "Reproducibility of the Sacred," 59.

80. Ruiz Gomar, "Virgin of Guadalupe," 160.

81. Ibid.

82. Peterson, "Virgin of Guadalupe," 158.

revelation, both figures violate their defined spaces. The varied gestures of the Virgin penetrate her mandorla to communicate with Juan Diego in the first two vignettes. Similarly, he eagerly extends his flower-filled mantle in the third vignette," partially obscuring the Guadalupe image.[83] This display of their personal interaction, Peterson says, "parallels the intimacy of their spoken dialogue, carried on in Nahuatl," in the work of Laso de la Vega.[84] It is not known whether Juárez was familiar with the work of Laso de la Vega (and, if he knew of it, whether he could read the Nahuatl text). However, this painting seems to evoke a sense of close connection between the Virgin and Juan Diego, which though present in Sánchez's work, is more evident in the work by Laso de la Vega.[85]

Finally, worthy of mention in this section are four full-page engravings by Matías de Arteaga y Alfaro (1630–1703), *Las cuatro apariciones* (The Four Apparitions). The illustrations accompanied the 1686 Sevillian publication of Luis Becerra Tanco's work, *La Felicidad de México* (Mexico's Joy). In these illustrations, Juan Diego appears to be "engaged in a sort of 'mystic dialogue' with a resplendent Virgin of Guadalupe framed by a garland of clouds."[86] Arteaga y Alfaro, much like Correa, abbreviates the written account of the apparitions and Jaime Cuadriello even speculates that Arteaga y Alfaro was familiar with and tried to replicate Correa's work.[87] These engravings by Arteaga y Alfaro gained great popularity and according to Cuadriello, "they were even reproduced in the monumental relief decor on the main façade of the old Basilica which opened in 1709."

The publication of *Imagen de la Virgen María* and *Huei tlamahuiçoltica* proved to be watershed moments in Guadalupan devotion, and with these two works the emphasis of artistic efforts in New Spain shifted as artists, no longer focusing solely on Guadalupe, aimed to image her apparitions to Juan Diego. There are a handful of known, quality examples of Guadalupe's apparitions at Tepeyac in the latter half of the seventeenth century. The works highlighted in this section of the essay typify this trend.

In addition to those images already discussed, similar examples can be added. First, Sánchez and others, like Becerra Tanco and Joseph Vidal de

---

83. Ibid.

84. Peterson, "Virgin of Guadalupe," 158.

85. In the *Nican mopohua*, the author uses poetic devices and the diminutive form to communicate a sense of intimacy between Juan Diego and the Virgin.

86. Cuadriello, "Marian Apparitions," 61.

87. Ibid.

Figueroa, who published books, leaflets, and sermons about Guadalupe in the later half of the seventeenth century, used images of the Virgin to accompany their written word.[88] Likewise, in "Iconología Guadalupana," Vargas Lugo makes mention of several known rudimentary representations of Guadalupe painted on wood dated to the seventeenth century. In one of the works she highlights, Guadalupe is pictured with Indian donors and in the other she is pictured with Juan Diego. These works are relevant because they show the diversity of artistic interpretation of the Guadalupe story. They provide evidence that not only Spanish and *criollo* peoples venerated the Virgin; those of lower social strata, mulattos and Indians, worshiped her as well.[89] The diversity of interpretation of Our Lady of Guadalupe and the apparition scenes indicates that there was a belief that she was unique and not meant to stay on the periphery.

CONCLUSION

The edict of 1637 issued by the ecclesiastical council of the cathedral of Mexico, coupled with other evidence from this century, speaks to the popularity of Guadalupe and the growth of Guadalupan devotion. The edict is relevant for those who study Our Lady of Guadalupe because it reveals that the devotion was widespread enough to cause controversy. Throughout the course of this essay, I have highlighted and explored the beliefs prevalent before and after the issuing of the edict. If Guadalupe had been inconsequential, the hierarchy of the Roman Catholic Church in New Spain would have left the issue alone—reproductions of her image could have appeared in any fashion whatsoever—for, bigger concerns were weighing on their souls during this epoch: the salvation of the natives. However, this was not the case. Guadalupe had gained enough prominence as a venerated image of the Virgin that the curia needed to preoccupy themselves with how she was being imaged and what beliefs were being propagated through such visual representations.

---

88. For example, an engraving of the third apparition is included in a book of Novenas authored by Sánchez dedicated to la Virgen de los Remedios and Guadalupe. For more information on this engraving, see Vargas Lugo, "Iconología Guadalupana," 73. In Figueroa's work, an image of the Virgin is accompanied by two vignettes of apparition scenes. See Peterson, "Virgin of Guadalupe," 157. The artist Antonio Castro's works were featured in several leaflets and in an edition of *La Felicidad de Mexico* by Becerra Tanco (1675). For an explanation of the importance of his interpretations of Guadalupe and the apparition accounts, see Vargas Lugo "Iconología Guadalupana," 74–75.

89. These images are in Vargas Lugo, "Iconología Guadalupana," 78–79.

These early pieces of art are crucial in understanding the development of Guadalupan devotion, as they both fostered and chronicled its evolution. In the span of fifty years, between the work of Echave Orio (1606) and the piece by Juárez (1656), one can assert that the devotion went from a local one specifically focused on the image of Guadalupe herself to a devotion with international adherents, attentive to Guadalupe and her apparitions to Juan Diego. The art, like the pieces by Juárez and Correa, sought to catechize the faithful and teach the viewer the story of Guadalupe. They provided a visual introduction to the tradition. Like the written accounts, the artwork aimed "to foster among the faithful a deeper devotion to Guadalupe's wondrous appearance, her maternal care, and her ongoing presence in her miraculous image."[90]

The pieces of artwork featured in this essay fill a void in what is known about the beliefs popular among early Guadalupan devotees. The art indicates undoubtedly that the faithful in New Spain believed in Guadalupe's divine origins, as evidenced in the work by Echave Orio, and moreover, they believed in her capacity to affect miracles, as seen in the Stradanus engraving. The art testifies that these beliefs existed decades before the publication of Sánchez's and Laso de la Vega's works. Future research and attention is needed in this area to determine more specifically *how* early these beliefs existed. If it is feasible to make such a determination from art, especially by focusing more on everyday Guadalupan art, like the pieces highlighted in Vargas Lugo's work, it may be possible to unveil even more insights into the contours and evolution of the Guadalupe tradition.

By placing these early art pieces in conversation with the earliest written works of the Guadalupan tradition and other historical events of the seventeenth century, it is possible to see what qualities enabled Guadalupe to rise above the other prominent images of the Virgin in New Spain. Through art, one can better understand how, of the multiple images of Mary circulating at the time, Guadalupe eventually became the principal image of the Virgin. Guadalupe's divine origins, her ability to intercede on the behalf of and offer protection to her faithful, and her role in salvation history, all helped her to become, in the following centuries, the *Reina de las Americas*.

90. Matovina, "First Pastoral Guadalupan Manual."

Figure I: *La Virgen de Guadalupe*, Juan de Correa, ca. 1667. Oil on canvas. 300 x 256 cm. Museo Nacional de Escultura, Valladolid, Spain. Ministerio de Educación, Cultura y Deporte (CE1679). This image is representative of the evolution in Guadalupan art in the seventeenth century, as it shows the apparitions of the Virgin to Juan Diego and the miraculous appearance of Our Lady of Guadalupe on the *tilma*.

Figure II: *Indulgence for alms toward the erection of a church dedicated to the Virgin of Guadalupe*, Samuel Stradanus, ca. 1613–1615. Copper Engraving. 32.7 x 20.9 cm. The Metropolitan Museum of Art, Gift of H. H. Behrens, 1948 (48.70).

Figure III: Stradanus detail featuring Catharina de Niehta.

BIBLIOGRAPHY

Bargellini, Clara. "Originality and Invention in the Painting of New Spain." In *Painting the New World: Mexican Art and Life (1521–1821)*, edited by Donna Pierce, Rogelio Ruiz Gomar, and Clara Bargellini, 79–91. Denver: Denver Art Museum, 2004.

Burkhart, Louise. "'Here Is Another Marvel': Marian Miracle Narratives in a Nahuatl Manuscript." In *Spiritual Encounters: Interactions Between Christianity and Native Religions in Colonial America*, edited by Nicolas Griffiths and Fernando Cervantes, 91–115. Lincoln: University of Nebraska Press, 1999.

Chávez, Eduardo. *Our Lady of Guadalupe and Saint Juan Diego: The Historical Evidence*. Translated by Carmen Treviño and Veronica Montano. Lanham, Md.: Rowman & Littlefield, 2006.

Cuadriello, Jaime. "An Apocalyptic View: Visions from Patmos-Tenochtitlan—The Eagle Woman." In *Visiones de Guadalupe*. México, D.F.: Artes de México, 1995.

———. Introduction to Jaime Cuadriello et al., *La Reina de las Américas: Works of Art from the Museum of the Basílica De Guadalupe*. Chicago: Mexican Fine Arts Center Museum, 1996.

———. "Marian Apparitions: Matías de Arteaga y Alfaro." In *La Reina de las Américas: Works of Art from the Museum of the Basílica De Guadalupe*, 60–61. Chicago: Mexican Fine Arts Center Museum, 1996.

León Mariscal, Beatriz Berndt. "The Miracles: Samuel Stradanus." In *La Reina de Las Américas: Works of Art from the Museum of the Basílica de Guadalupe*. Chicago: Mexican Fine Arts Center Museum, 1996.

Matovina, Timothy. "The First Guadalupan Pastoral Manual: Luis Laso de la Vega's *Huei tlamahuiçoltica* (1649)." *Horizons: The Journal of the College Theology Society* 40 (2013) 159–77.

———. "Guadalupe at Calvary: Patristic Theology in Miguel Sánchez's *Imagen de la Virgen María* (1648)." *Theological Studies* 64 (2003) 795–811.

———. "Theologies of Guadalupe: From the Spanish Colonial Era to Pope John Paul II." *Theological Studies* 70 (2009) 61–91.

Peterson, Jeanette. "Canonizing a Cult: A Wonderworking Guadalupe for Seventeenth-Century Mexico." In *Religion and Society in New Spain*, edited by Stafford Poole and Susan Schroeder, 125–56. Albuquerque: University of New Mexico Press, 2007.

———. "The Reproducibility of the Sacred: Simulacra of the Virgin of Guadalupe." In *Exploring New World Imagery*, edited by Donna Pierce, 41–78. Denver: Denver Art Museum, 2005.

———. "The Virgin of Guadalupe with Apparitions by José Juarez [1656]." In *Painting the New World: Mexican Art and Life (1521–1821)*, edited by Donna Pierce, Rogelio Ruiz Gomar, and Clara Bargellini, 154–59. Denver: Denver Art Museum, 2004.

———. *Visualizing Guadalupe: From Black Madonna to Queen of the Americas*. Austin: University of Texas Press, 2014.

Poole, Stafford. *Our Lady of Guadalupe: The Origins and Sources of a Mexican National Symbol, 1531–1797*. Tucson: University of Arizona Press, 1995.

Ruiz Gomar, Rogelio. "The Virgin of Guadalupe with Apparitions by José Juarez [1656]." In *Painting the New World: Mexican Art and Life (1521–1821)*, edited by Donna Pierce, Rogelio Ruiz Gomar, and Clara Bargellini, 159–60. Denver: Denver Art Museum, 2004.

Sánchez, Miguel. *Imagen de la Virgen María, Madre de Dios de Guadalupe*. In *Testimonios históricos guadalupanos*, edited by Ernesto de la Torre Villar and Ramiro Navarro de Anda, 152–267. México City: Fondo de Cultura Económica, 1982.

Sousa, Lisa, Stafford Poole, and James Lockhart, eds. and trans. *The Story of Guadalupe: Luis Laso de la Vega's* Huei tlamahuiçoltica *of 1649*. Stanford: Stanford University Press, 1998.

Taylor, William B. "The Virgin of Guadalupe in New Spain: An Inquiry into the Social History of Marian Devotion." *American Ethnologist* 14.1 (1987) 9–33.

Vargas Lugo, Elisa. "Iconología Guadalupana." In *Imágenes Guadalupanas: Cuatro siglos*, 57–178. México City: Centro Cultural Arte Contemporaneo, 1987.

Wolf, Eric R. "The Virgin of Guadalupe: A Mexican National Symbol." *Journal of American Folklore* 71. (1958) 34–39.

4

The Huei tlamahuiçoltica
Responding to Pastoral Challenges in
Light of Our Lady of Guadalupe

Alison Fitchett Climenhaga

IN 1649, LUIS LASO de la Vega, a *criollo* diocesan priest of Mexico City, published his pastoral manual, the *Huei tlamahuiçoltica*. Written in the Nahuatl language, the manual was aimed at spreading devotion to Our Lady of Guadalupe, especially among the Nahuas of central Mexico. Although Laso de la Vega lived a century after the first Christian missionaries began to evangelize the region, he wrote and ministered against the backdrop of several pastoral challenges inherited from the initial evangelization: rampant death and social change among the Nahuas, uncertainty about how to identify an exemplary Christian life in New Spain, and difficulty communicating with the Nahua population. After examining sixteenth-century efforts to evangelize New Spain, this essay will argue that Laso de la Vega perceived and responded to these pastoral challenges and that this shaped the way he crafted his pastoral manual even as his experience of the Guadalupe event helped him formulate answers to these challenges. Laso de la Vega's decisions in molding his manual—including his decision to write it in Nahuatl—reflect his historical and social reality and signal some important themes in contemporary theology.

PASTORAL CHALLENGES IN THE EVANGELIZATION OF SIXTEENTH-CENTURY NEW SPAIN

In the wake of Hernán Cortés's conquest of Mexico, representatives of the mendicant religious orders began the work of evangelizing the inhabitants of the region. Pedro de Gante, a Franciscan of Flemish origin, arrived with two companions as early as 1523. The following year, a group of twelve Franciscan missionaries arrived and initiated "methodical evangelization."[1] They were quickly followed in 1526 by twelve Dominican missionaries and in 1533 by a party of Augustinians. These mendicant orders dominated early efforts to evangelize New Spain. But starting around 1550, the orders increasingly came into conflict and competition with the secular clergy. The mendicant orders exercised ordinary clerical authority in New Spain only during the process of initial evangelization. In keeping with the reforming efforts of the Council of Trent, established parishes came under the authority of the bishops, leaving the mendicants either to "submit to the jurisdiction of the bishops" or surrender their parishes to the secular clergy.[2] Despite concerns about the ability of the secular clergy to minister to the Nahuas—especially given that the secular clergy generally had less linguistic training than the mendicants—by the 1580s they had largely replaced the mendicants ministering to the Christian Nahuas of central Mexico.

Many of the early missionaries hoped to establish an ideal Christian society in the New World, free of the decadence and depravity that had corrupted the church in the Old World.[3] An engraving from Diego de Valadés's *Rhetorica Christiana* (1579) symbolically depicts this idea: twelve Franciscan friars arrive in the New World carrying Saint Peter's Basilica on their shoulders, intent on re-founding the church there.[4] To reach this goal, the missionaries sought to minister to the Nahuas and form them into good Christians. Accomplishing this apostolic work necessitated learning about Nahua language, history, culture, and religion, for without this knowledge they could not hope to communicate the Christian message effectively or to

---

1. Ricard, *Spiritual Conquest of Mexico*, 21.
2. Ibid., 109. See also Burkhart, *Slippery Earth*, 18–19.
3. For more on the utopian and messianic ideals of the mendicant orders, see Jacques Lafaye, *Quetzalcóatl and Guadalupe*, esp. chaps. 3 and 4. Similarly, in *Origins of Mexican Catholicism*, Osvaldo Pardo discusses the way in which these ideals and the methods of evangelization that flowed from them were rooted in different conceptions of the primitive church; see esp. his introduction and chap. 1.
4. For a copy of the image, see Lara, *Christian Texts*, 66.

recognize and correct the errors they perceived in the Nahua social and religious system. In collaboration with indigenous assistants, the missionaries set about performing what we now recognize as ethnographic research to learn about the inhabitants of the New World.[5] Their linguistic work in particular constituted an important contribution to the evangelization project, for it put vital information in the hands of their fellow missionaries who were less linguistically adept.[6] Although their cultural assumptions, religious convictions, and missionary goals colored the subjects that interested them and how they assessed Nahua society, they succeeded in collecting data that laid a foundation for catechizing the Nahuas.

As the missionaries learned about Nahua life, they tried to discern the extent to which Christianity conflicted with or was prefigured by the Nahua past associated with pagan worship. Understanding this relationship emerged as a concern because of the seeming parallels between Nahua and Christian religious rituals and symbols. When missionaries saw things that looked like crosses, they speculated that these might have had their origin in Christian practice. Similarly, learning of the existence of a Nahua ritual in which an individual confessed moral failing and received absolution, some missionaries concluded that the Nahuas not only had a concept of sin similar to that of European Christians but also practiced a rudimentary form of the sacrament of penance to cleanse themselves.

The missionaries accounted for these similarities in several ways.[7] One was to attribute them to demonic activity aimed at deceiving the Nahuas into performing (and the missionaries into permitting or even encouraging) idolatrous worship. A second explanation credited the resemblances to a prior evangelization of the New World which introduced a Christianity that had grown increasingly distorted over time. Here, interpretation of the Great Commission functioned as the key to interpreting the Nahua past. The missionaries wrestled with the biblical portrayal of Christ's commandment to his disciples to make disciples of all nations (Matt 28:16–20). Did this indicate that the disciples literally took the Christian message to the ends of the earth? If so, they must have reached the New World sometime in the distant past. If, on the other hand, the mendicants interpreted the passage as a mandate entrusted to both the disciples and their successors,

5. Ricard, *Spiritual Conquest*, 39–60.

6. Ibid., 48.

7. See Pardo, *Origins of Mexican Catholicism*, 89–90; Lafaye, *Quetzalcóatl and Guadalupe*, 44–50.

they could imagine themselves as the first evangelizers of the New World, partaking in the apostolic preaching task. Finally, some missionaries argued that any similarities between Christianity and Nahua religion were the fruit of God's grace at work among the Nahuas in advance of any missionary proclamation.

How the missionaries perceived the origins of Nahua religiosity impacted their approach to incorporating its symbols and thought into the Christianity they taught. Could the seeming similarities between Nahua and Christian religion serve as a basis for preaching Christianity? Or did they need to present Christianity as a radical break from anything the Nahuas knew from their own religious system? Even when missionaries stressed the discontinuity of Christianity and Nahua religion, in practice they often simultaneously preserved certain indigenous ways of thinking or acting. Perhaps the ultimate symbol of Christian triumphalism in New Spain came in the form of constructing Christian churches on the sites of destroyed Aztec temples, often incorporating stones from the former temples into the new churches. While the missionaries intended to convey through this the supremacy of Christianity over pagan religion, in important ways they effectively cultivated a sense of continuity between religious systems. For rather than entirely disrupting the Nahuas' sense of sacred geography, this practice enabled them to continue worshipping at the same holy sites. Thus the practice was far more ambiguous than most missionaries would have liked to admit. Jaime Lara contends that "much less of the pre-Hispanic religion was destroyed, and much more was recycled, because it was relatively easily Christianized (or was it that Christianity was relatively easily indigenized and mestizized?)"[8]

Urgency of the Sacraments amid Rampant Death

In their quest to convert and catechize the Nahuas, the missionaries faced a number of challenges that threatened the success of their pastoral work. First of all, with the arrival of the Spanish conquistadors and missionaries came rampant death and depopulation of the Nahuas, caused by both violent conquest and epidemics. This posed a grave threat to the missionaries' overarching goal for New Spain, for creating a model Christian society would be difficult if many of its potential members were dying. Moreover, these circumstances gave particular urgency to the administration of the

---

8. Lara, *Christian Texts*, 262.

sacraments: the salvation of the souls of the dying was at stake, so administering the sacraments—especially baptism—as quickly as possible to the greatest number of people was imperative.

Expediting the administration of baptism posed several challenges. First of all, the missionaries debated how much catechesis the Nahuas needed to have before they could receive the sacraments.[9] In 1555, the First Mexican Church Council mandated that every adult baptismal candidate receive catechetical instruction prior to baptism, but the mendicant orders ministering in Mexico interpreted this need for catechesis in different ways. The Dominicans and Augustinians tended to view catechesis as the means by which converts could experience "informed participation . . . in the ritual."[10] On the other hand, the Franciscans emphasized catechesis as part of an ongoing process of instruction which served to develop an interpersonal relationship between the Nahuas, who needed tutelage, and the priests, who supervised them and provided an example of Christian living. Throughout the process, the priests relied heavily on Nahua catechists—often particularly adept children singled out for special instruction—who could earn the trust of and communicate more easily with their fellow Nahuas than the missionaries could.[11] Collaboration like this was essential to the success of the evangelization project, especially in the early years when relatively few missionaries were available to minister to the Nahua population.

The missionaries also debated the degree to which they could adapt the baptismal rite to suit their pastoral situation. In the context of the mass baptisms that seemed the only effective way to administer baptism to the numerous Nahuas in need of salvific grace, they deliberated about which elements of the ritual were essential to the sacrament.[12] Some, especially Franciscans, tended to minimize the ritual elements, while others sought to uphold the solemnity of the full baptismal rite. Still others advocated performing the most essential rites, such as exorcism, baptism with water, and anointing with chrism, on all baptismal candidates while selecting a few representatives upon whom to perform the remaining rites. Some missionaries experimented with incorporating Nahua religious symbols and objects into the baptismal

9. For the debates surrounding pre-baptismal catechesis, see Pardo, *Origins of Mexican Catholicism*, 43–48.

10. Ibid., 47.

11. Ricard, *Spiritual Conquest of Mexico*, 97–101; Lara, *Christian Texts*, 60–62; Trexler, "From the Mouths of Babes," in *Church and Community*.

12. Pardo, *Origins of Mexican Catholicism*, 20–38; Ricard, *Spiritual Conquest*, 91–95; Lara, *Christian Texts*, 80–90.

rite. For instance, Franciscan Gerónimo de Mendieta promoted adapting the rite for infants to Nahua society by incorporating some of the objects associated with local infant naming rituals. Traditionally, after a ritual bath to cleanse them from impurity, Nahua infants were named and given tiny arrows (for boys) or brooms (for girls), which signaled their future martial and domestic duties. Mendieta proposed including these symbols in Christian baptism "to indicate that the newly baptized have to fight in a manly way against the enemies of their souls, and have to sweep [their souls] clean of any filth and prepare a clean dwelling place for Christ in their hearts."[13] Others daringly converted pre-Christian statues and calendar stones into baptismal fonts. Through such measures the missionaries hoped to make Christianity attractive to and comprehensible for the Nahuas, as well as practical for the priests to administer, so that as many Nahuas as possible could be baptized into the faith.

Conceptualizing a Christian Life in a New Cultural Context

The missionaries all agreed that they wanted to form these Nahuas, imperiled body and soul, into Christians. But they struggled to know how to recognize and inculcate a good Christian life among the Nahuas, for there was no consensus about what a Christian life would look like in this new setting. They emphasized the need for catechetical instruction, but the doctrinal content of this instruction was minimal, consisting primarily of learning a few prayers like the *Pater Noster* and *Ave Maria*, the Ten Commandments, and the fourteen Articles of Faith.[14] Instead of emphasizing doctrine, the missionaries focused their attention on teaching the Nahuas how to behave like Christians, for they believed that it was "more important that the Indians lead a simple, Christian life than that they understand Christian doctrine on a metaphysical and philosophical level."[15] To this end, they drew on stories of Jesus and the saints to provide models of Christian moral behavior.[16]

As the missionaries understood it, one of the most essential aspects of the Christian life they sought to cultivate was Christian worship. Because of this they poured a great deal of energy into teaching the Nahuas how to

13. Quoted in Lara, *Christian Texts*, 83.
14. Ricard, *Spiritual Conquest*, 101–2.
15. Burkhart, *Slippery Earth*, 10.
16. Ibid., 25.

enact right worship. Indeed, witnessing and participating in worship was itself perceived as having a catechetical function, making it the "best way to inculcate the faith in new believers."[17] Through the pomp and spectacle of public worship, the missionaries hoped to draw the Nahuas into the Christian faith and override their devotion to non-Christian deities at their domestic altars.[18] Whether through celebrating Mass, administering sacraments, or organizing liturgical dramas, the missionaries sought "to win less the hearts and minds than the knees" of the Nahuas, for they judged the success of the missionary enterprise "not by the assimilation of ideas but by the natives' physical and verbal comportment."[19] As they tried to bring about religious transformation in the New World, they relied on external indicators involving action and deportment to gauge—and effect—change in the Nahuas' religious world.

Linguistic Challenges and the Choice to Use Nahuatl

In order for worship and catechesis to have this transformative effect, the missionaries needed to be able to communicate with the Nahuas. But given the sheer linguistic and cultural diversity that characterized New Spain, communication was fraught with difficulty. Since the missionaries wanted to preach their message, judge converts' sincerity, and administer the sacraments, an absence of communication constituted an obstacle to the Nahuas' salvation. As such, the missionaries strove to overcome this obstacle. They organized liturgical dramas that enacted stories from salvation history and gave the Nahuas a chance to identify with those stories by having them act the stories out themselves.[20] They also engaged in visual preaching: pointing to images to illustrate a sermon, or delivering a sermon with a fresco as a backdrop for dramatic effect.[21] Nevertheless, they had to master the art of verbal communication with the Nahuas to give a full account of the Christian message and persuade the Nahuas to adopt it.

Many of the earliest missionaries were chosen for their linguistic aptitude, and learning the local language was among their first priorities. Once they knew the language, they set about translating catechetical material and

17. Lara, *Christian Texts*, 15. See also Ricard, *Spiritual Conquest*, 176–93.
18. Trexler, "We Think, They Act," in *Church and Community*, 582.
19. Ibid., 580.
20. Ibid., Lara, *Christian Texts*, 201–28.
21. Lara, *Christian Texts*, 48–56.

portions of the Bible into the vernacular. Moreover, they began to use local rhetorical forms and modes of expression in their writing and preaching, as a strategy to persuade their audience to embrace the truth of their message.[22] But their investigation and appropriation of vernacular vocabulary and forms was selective, for it was driven by the need to communicate particular Christian concepts. Even the missionaries' choice of which local languages to learn and use was selective. When Cortés arrived, over eighty languages or dialects were extant in New Spain.[23] Nahuatl was most widely used because the Aztec empire had introduced it across the region to facilitate trade and governance. The missionaries adopted Nahuatl as the primary means of communicating with the people to whom they ministered, for given the constraints of time and limited resources they needed to find one language capable of communicating with as many people as possible. It is true that as the missionaries moved outward from central Mexico into areas where Nahuatl was less prevalent, they increasingly needed to learn other vernaculars, as well.[24] But ultimately, in their quest to communicate meaningfully with the Nahua people, the missionaries took a local lingua franca, Nahuatl, and, by adapting and spreading it, increased its hegemony in the region.

This choice was a source of controversy. Some, like King Charles V, expressed concerns about the language's ability to convey the mysteries of the Christian faith adequately.[25] The decision to use Nahuatl also ran afoul of the Spanish Crown's attempts to Hispanicize New Spain. Against the backdrop of the Catholic monarchs' practice of spreading the use of Castilian throughout the Iberian Peninsula during the Reconquista, Castilian had become associated with membership in the Spanish Catholic Empire. For much of the sixteenth century the monarchs insisted that the church in New Spain conduct its instruction in Castilian instead of, or at least alongside, Nahuatl. But the missionaries resisted, protesting that this was neither practical, since teaching Castilian would require neglecting subjects indispensable to the Nahuas' conversion, nor desirable, for a language barrier

22. Burkhart, *Slippery Earth*, 11–14, 189–90.

23. Heath, *Telling Tongues*, 3.

24. For a summary of the languages the missionaries used, see Ricard, *Spiritual Conquest*, 46–48.

25. Heath, *Telling Tongues*, 19. For more on the Spanish Crown's often contradictory linguistic policy for New Spain and the responses of the missionaries, see Ricard, *Spiritual Conquest*, 50–52; Heath, *Telling Tongues*, 1–36; Pardo, *Origins of Mexican Catholicism*, 109–10.

the huei tlamahuiçoltica

would help protect the Nahuas from the corrupting influence of Europeans. Moreover, the missionaries believed that the Nahuas were incapable of assimilating the Castilian language. They resisted conducting catechesis in Castilian because they did not want to limit potential converts to the few capable of mastering the new language. To support their position, the missionaries argued that Nahuatl could indeed express Christian truth adequately, and that it was the most effective medium for leading the Nahuas to adopt Christianity. In practice, Spanish settlers and colonial officials supported the missionaries, fearing that teaching the Nahuas Castilian would give them too much power in society.

In 1570, King Philip II reluctantly concluded that using Nahuatl was necessary to promote conversion to Christianity, and he issued a series of edicts declaring Nahuatl the "official language" of the indigenous population, ordering educational institutions to offer courses in the language, and mandating that clerics who worked in New Spain know it.[26] By the time Laso de la Vega published the *Huei tlamahuiçoltica*, all clerics in New Spain were at least nominally required to have competence in Nahuatl or in other local languages. But the frequency with which Philip and his son were forced to remind secular and ecclesial officials of the importance of learning the vernacular implies that, in practice, many priests failed to comply with the Crown's orders.

RESPONDING TO PASTORAL CHALLENGES THROUGH THE HUEI TLAMAHUIÇOLTICA

Writing in the seventeenth century, Luis Laso de la Vega ministered in a substantially different situation than that faced by the sixteenth-century missionaries. Social upheaval among the Nahuas had lessened, and the missionaries' linguistic and cultural competency had improved. Yet Laso de la Vega still encountered many of the same pastoral challenges either directly or indirectly. In responding to them, his focus differed from that of his predecessors, however. In contrast with earlier missionaries, the questions he sought to address in his pastoral manual, the *Huei tlamahuiçoltica*, focus less on how to administer the sacraments to the Nahuas and more on how to encourage popular devotions among them.[27]

26. Heath, *Telling Tongues*, 26–27.

27. The sacraments were not unimportant to Laso de la Vega. As will be further discussed below, the manual highlights Juan Diego frequently going to confession and

73

Laso de la Vega became the vicar of the sanctuary at Tepeyac dedicated to Our Lady of Guadalupe in 1647. Two years later, he published the *Huei tlamahuiçoltica*, written in Nahuatl. As a pastoral manual, it is part of a broader genre of texts intended to assist with pastoral work. Containing collections of liturgical texts, guidelines for administering the sacraments, instructions about which steps to take in particular pastoral circumstances, and sometimes even visual aids, these manuals helped bridge the gap between abstract theological reflection and concrete pastoral applications. In New Spain, these aids helped priests and catechists ministering to people with religious, cultural, and linguistic backgrounds often radically different from their own.

In a similar vein, the *Huei tlamahuiçoltica* contains narrative material and theological reflection useful for both catechetical and liturgical purposes. The manual opens with an introductory preface addressed to the Virgin in which the author outlines his purpose for writing.[28] Next comes the *Nican mopohua*, which describes the apparitions of the Virgin to Juan Diego, tells of how Guadalupe's image came to be imprinted on Juan Diego's *tilma*, and gives a short description of the image. The *Nican motecpana* contains a series of miracle accounts, providing examples of both Spanish and Nahua devotees of Guadalupe calling out to her in situations of need and receiving her assistance. These stories are followed by a short narrative about Juan Diego, who spent the remainder of his days near the sanctuary at Tepeyac, leading a life of pious devotion. The *Nican tlantica* concludes the manual by reflecting on Guadalupe's identity and significance as a manifestation of the Virgin Mary, the mother of Jesus. Finally, appended to the end of the manual is a "prayer to be directed to the heavenly Queen, our precious mother of Guadalupe" (127).[29] Likely, this prayer was intended to serve as a model for Guadalupe's devotees.

Scholars debate the authorship of the text, suggesting that Laso de la Vega may have either published the work of Nahua assistants or compiled and reprinted earlier works.[30] Regardless of the degree to which Laso de

---

communion. This is part of what marks him as a good and faithful Christian. Similarly, the dying Juan Bernardino requests his nephew bring a friar to hear his confession.

28. For a theological analysis of *Huei tlamahuiçoltica*, see Matovina, "First Guadalupan Pastoral Manual."

29. All parenthetical page numbers refer to the *Huei tlamahuiçoltica* text contained in Sousa et al., *Story of Guadalupe*.

30. For discussion of the authorship of the manual, see Sousa et al., *Story of Guadalupe*, 1–47 (esp. 18–21 and 43–47). See also Brading, *Mexican Phoenix*, 91–92, 352, and

la Vega was directly engaged in composing each portion of the text, it seems clear that at minimum he authored the introduction, which contains important clues about the theological worldview that oriented his project of publishing the Nahuatl pastoral manual. Moreover, even if he published under his own name the work done by his assistants or earlier materials related to the Guadalupe event, the fact that he compiled and disseminated this material says something about his theological commitments and the needs he perceived in his concrete pastoral situation. Hence it will be assumed here that material in the manual reflects Laso de la Vega's basic theological orientation.

To Enhance Devotion and Keep Guadalupe's Memory Alive

Laso de la Vega's primary purpose in publishing the manual, as the text states it, is to make known throughout New Spain the great deeds of Guadalupe and thereby enhance devotion to her. Laso de la Vega expresses his wish that the "humble commoners" will "see here and find out in their language all the charitable acts you have performed on their behalf" (55). He laments that too often in the past people have been mindful of the benevolence and greatness of Guadalupe only when in immediate need, "only at the very moment when they have obtained them do they wonder at and give thanks for the favors of the heavenly Queen, but soon they cast them into oblivion, so that those who come afterward in attaining the light of the sun of our Lord arrive too late for them" (117; see also 55). He has two concerns here. The first is a general human tendency to forget one's ongoing dependence upon divine aid soon after a pressing need is met. Building upon this, he also worries that the memory of Guadalupe has faded over time. Writing a century after the 1531 date he assigns to Guadalupe's appearance at Tepeyac, he fears that much knowledge has already been lost, "erased" by time "because the ancients did not take care to write it down when it happened" (117). In response, he hopes to bring knowledge of and devotion to Guadalupe to the forefront of Christian consciousness in New Spain.

The manual itself was poised to play an important role in this process, for its primary audience would have been priests engaged in pastoral work among the Nahuas.[31] The various components of the manual, particularly the *Nican mopohua* narrative and the miracle testimonies, provided raw

---

358–60.

31. Matovina, "First Guadalupan Pastoral Manual."

material that they could draw on when preaching to and catechizing their flock. Also, while the manual contains the extended narrative of the Guadalupe apparitions in the *Nican mopohua*, the main events and themes of the narrative are reiterated in summary form several times throughout the rest of the *Huei tlamahuiçoltica*. For example, the narrative is woven into a description, contained within the miracle accounts of the *Nican motecpana*, of the origins and miraculous properties of the spring near the sanctuary at Tepeyac. The passage describes how the spring is located in the place where the Virgin intercepted Juan Diego when he was preoccupied with tending to his sick uncle, showed him where she desired her temple to be built, instructed him to cut the miraculous flowers, and commanded him to bring them to the bishop as a sign. Similarly, the prayer at the end of the text recounts Guadalupe's apparition and describes appropriate forms of devotion to her in abbreviated form. These shorter units would have served as important catechetical material for introducing the Nahuas to the story of Guadalupe.

The *Huei tlamahuiçoltica* and Salvation in the Midst of Affliction

The cataclysmic depopulation wrought among the Nahuas had abated considerably by the mid-seventeenth century, and the indigenous population had started to stabilize, albeit at a greatly diminished number. But Laso de la Vega and his fellow priests ministered to a population that was still reeling from the experience of a century of violent conquest and social upheaval. Consciously or not, the text of the *Huei tlamahuiçoltica* manifests this in several ways. First of all, the *Nican mopohua* reflects some of the psychological and social consequences of conquest when it portrays Juan Diego as having a negative self-image. After his first audience with Bishop Juan de Zumárraga, in which Juan Diego is unable to convince the bishop of the truth of his message, Juan Diego returns to the Virgin and asks her to send another more worthy messenger:

> For I am a poor ordinary man, I carry burdens with the tumpline and carrying frame, I am one of the common people, one who is governed. Where you are sending me is not my usual place ... Pardon me if I cause you concern, if I incur or bring upon myself your frown or your wrath. (69–71)[32]

32. In Virgilio Elizondo's translation of the *Nican mopohua* in his *Guadalupe: Mother of the New Creation*, Juan Diego's language is even more striking: "Because in reality I am

the huei tlamahuiçoltica

His self-deprecations indicate that he has internalized his conquerors' ideas about his own unworthiness. The way the servants of the bishop belittle Juan Diego and strive to turn the bishop against him further reinforces this theme (67, 73–75, 81).

The manual also reflects a situation in which illness and affliction were pervasive, ongoing threats to the people of New Spain. One of the miracles Guadalupe performs in the apparition account is the healing of Juan Diego's uncle, Juan Bernardino. Similarly, the *Nican motecpana* miracle testimonies revolve primarily around devotees who petition the Virgin to heal them from various ailments that threaten their well-being. One miracle story makes explicit reference to the epidemics that had ravaged the population during the previous century. It describes an epidemic of 1544 responsible for killing over a hundred people each day, saying that "our Lord the giver of life was reducing and depopulating the land" (95). God's "ire and wrath" against the people subsided only when they invoked the compassionate intercession of Guadalupe. The Nahuas would have immediately identified with the petitioners in these accounts, for they faced similar afflictions and were well aware of the fragility of life. The text encourages the demoralized, presenting devotion to Guadalupe as the solution to the pain of their physical and social condition.

The manual uses multiple strategies to showcase the Virgin as an effective remedy. One of the principle themes running throughout the text is that Guadalupe defends those in need. It repeatedly affirms that she comes especially on behalf of those who are poor and downtrodden. Linking Guadalupe with the wider tradition of Marian veneration, the text stresses that all over the world, the Virgin Mary "herself has chosen out and set up her dwelling places and her images so that there she may help the needy who should come into her presence" (119). It goes on to highlight the particular favor that Mary has demonstrated for the indigenous people through the Guadalupe apparition:

> Especially she about whom we are speaking set up her residence here at Tepeyacac and by a great miracle gave her people her image . . . Although she now helps all different kinds of people who in their affliction come to greet her in her home, let the local people,

---

one of those campesinos, a piece of rope, a small ladder, the excrement of people; I am a leaf; they order me around, lead me by force; and you, my most abandoned Daughter, my Child, my Lady, and my Queen, send me to a place where I do not belong. Forgive me, I will cause pain to your countenance and to your heart; I will displease you and fall under your wrath, my Lady, and my owner," 10.

> the humble commoners, be sure that it was for their very sake that their Queen condescended to house herself there. (121)

The Virgin also concretely demonstrates her love for the downtrodden in her interactions with Juan Diego. When he protests his unworthiness for the favor she has shown him and the mission with which she as entrusted him, she gently corrects him by affirming his dignity. She assures him that she did not choose her messenger from among "high ranking people" and that "it is highly necessary that you yourself be involved and take care of it" (71). She refuses to allow Juan Diego to evade his vocation as a child of God and one singled out for her service.

Similarly, although the bishop and his servants initially fail to accept Juan Diego as a trustworthy messenger, by the end of the apparition narrative they repent and respect him. After the image of the Virgin appears on the *tilma*, the bishop hosts Juan Diego (and later also his uncle, Juan Bernardino) in his palace, and he allows Juan Diego to lead him to the hilltop at Tepeyac where the Virgin desires her temple to be built. Later, when Juan Diego requests permission to live at Tepeyac so that he can better serve the Virgin in her sanctuary, the bishop grants him a small house, "for the lord bishop esteemed him very highly" (113). In the course of the story, Juan Diego shifts from one whose word is suspect to one honored as the agent through whom the bishop, his household, and eventually people throughout the region come to know of and become devoted to Guadalupe. Together with the portrayals of Guadalupe as an efficacious healer and defender of the dignity of the poor, the text's overarching message is that devotion to Guadalupe is a potent remedy for all the troubles one might face in daily life.

The *Huei tlamahuiçoltica*: Towards a Model of Christian Life

Aware of the importance of fostering Christian discipleship in New Spain, Laso de la Vega positions his manual to respond to concerns about inculcating an exemplary Christian life among the Nahuas. Through multiple illustrations of how devotees ought to respond to Guadalupe, he endeavors to show what a model Christian life entails. The miracle accounts graphically depict the appropriate response to the Virgin, as well as the fruits of that response. While Laso de la Vega includes testimonies about a wide array of different miracles Guadalupe has performed, each uses essentially the same simple formula as its basis: a need (often a crisis involving the health or safety of one or more devotees) impels someone to call on Guadalupe for help, and she swiftly responds by defending her devotees from whatever affliction they face.[33] They, in turn, display deep gratitude and increased devotion to her. For instance, during a procession celebrating the completion of the sanctuary at Tepeyac and the transfer of her image there, an arrow wounds a Nahua man in the neck (93). His relatives quickly take his lifeless body before Guadalupe's image and cry out to her for help. She immediately revives him and heals the wound, leaving only a scar. The crowd marvels and praises the Virgin, and the man devotes his life to serving in her sanctuary. Occasionally, the Virgin takes charge of the situation before her people even have time to seek her aid, as when she protects a man praying in her sanctuary from harm when a heavy lamp falls on his head (103). After the fact, her devotees credit her with averting the crisis.

Often the miracle accounts model specific devotional practices. For instance, during an epidemic in 1544, the Franciscan friars organize a penitential procession of young children, who walk along flogging themselves and calling on Guadalupe to intercede on their behalf (95). A woman with a swollen stomach has herself carried to the Tepeyac sanctuary on a litter, and she prostrates herself before the image of the Virgin to pray for healing (107). Similarly, another woman suffering from hydropsy visits the sanctuary to pray and drink from the spring that flows from the hillside there (109). As she swallows the water, she experiences healing. Although some of these practices may seem peculiar to contemporary sensibilities, each image would have provided examples to the Nahuas of how to comport themselves as Christians, for they illustrated specific recognizably Christian behaviors that the Nahuas could imitate.

The portrayal of Juan Diego himself stands out as the premier model of Christian devotion in the *Huei tlamahuiçoltica*. In the narrative, he always obeys the Virgin's instructions, sometimes at great personal risk and cost. He goes to the bishop's palace to deliver the Virgin's message, although he knows the bishop will doubt him. There, he experiences mockery at the hands of the bishop's servants. When his uncle is dying, Juan Diego gives up the search for a confessor in order to do the Virgin's bidding, having faith in her promise to heal Juan Bernardino. Moreover, after the sanctuary is

---

33. This is a familiar formula in Peninsular devotional traditions. For example, a number of the miracle accounts in Gonzalo de Berceo's *Miracles of Our Lady (Milagros de Nuestra Señora)*, a thirteenth-century compilation of *exempla*, have a similar structure, especially the *exempla* of The Simple Cleric, The Prior and Uberto the Sexton, and The Pregnant Abbess.

constructed at Tepeyac, Juan Diego spends the rest of his days in an ascetic life of devotion to Guadalupe. Leaving his property to Juan Bernardino, he spends his time alone, praying to her and tending her sanctuary (113). Even the end of his life is exemplary. On his deathbed, she comes to him in a dream, and upon his passing "the consummate Virgin and her precious child took his soul to where it would enjoy completely the happiness of heaven" (115). The account ends with an invocation expressing the author's desire that "it be her wish that we too may serve her and abandon all the worldly things that lead us astray, so that we too may attain the eternal riches of heaven" (115). The implication is clear: those who imitate Juan Diego in his devotion to Guadalupe can expect to enjoy the same celestial reward. Through his humility, lifelong fidelity, and his willingness to sacrifice on her behalf, Juan Diego becomes a paradigm of Christian virtue, worthy of the imitation not only of Nahua but also Spanish Christians.

Laso de la Vega recognizes Juan Diego's exemplary indigenous response to Guadalupe through categories familiar to him from traditional Catholic Marian devotion. As Timothy Matovina points out, the text casts Juan Diego "as a model Franciscan lay brother or lay person living a consecrated life."[34] Not only does he devote his life to prayer and solitude at the shrine, he also would frequently "go to confession and communion, fast, do penance, punish himself, and gird himself with a sharp metal net" (113). Moreover, the text claims that he had never had sexual relations with a woman, for he and his wife, who died two years before the Virgin appeared, lived in a chaste marriage in response to a sermon preached by a Franciscan missionary. In the above examples, European expectations about holiness deeply shaped the characterization of Juan Diego's person and piety. At the same time, the choice to portray an indigenous person embodying these characteristics is itself significant, for it was by no means taken for granted that those born in the New World—Nahua or *criollo*—were capable of attaining the same spiritual maturity of those born in Europe.

Laso de la Vega's Decision to Write in Nahuatl

Laso de la Vega also engages the issue of communication barriers between missionaries and the indigenous peoples with whom they desired to share the Christian message. In response to the challenge of communicating with the Nahuas in a way that made the message attractive and comprehensible,

---

34. Matovina, "First Guadalupan Pastoral Manual," 169.

the huei tlamahuiçoltica

he elects to write his pastoral manual in Nahuatl. Many of the reasons for this choice are practical. Even after a century of Spanish presence in the New World, many Nahuas were not proficient in Castilian. Thus, catechizing them in a local tongue was imperative. The text of the *Huei tlamahuiçoltica* reflects Laso de la Vega's awareness of this. In his preface, he attributes his decision to write in Nahuatl to his desire to make Guadalupe and her marvelous deeds known among the Nahuas. Addressing the Virgin, he expresses his intent that "the humble commoners" will "see here and find out in their language all the charitable acts you have performed on their behalf" (55). Also worth recalling is the fact that a substantial portion of Laso de la Vega's audience consisted of his fellow priests, many of whom would not have been fluent in Nahuatl. A manual like this provided catechetical material for these priests to draw upon to assist in their ministry. It would have especially helped those less proficient in Nahuatl, for they could utilize sections of the text rather than struggling to compose their own original material.

Inculcating knowledge of Guadalupe is crucial for Laso de la Vega due to the role he assigns her in the history of New Spain, for he considers her appearance and subsequent devotion to her as decisive factors in the evangelization effort both during the sixteenth century and in his own time. As his treatise portrays it, after her image is enshrined at the sanctuary at Tepeyac, a great flood of people rush there to see what had happened: "There was a movement in all the altepetls everywhere of people coming to see and marvel at her precious image. They came to show their devotion and pray to her" (89). The apparition narrative and image attracts the people to Tepeyac, where they are drawn into devotion to the Virgin. Indeed, this was precisely the purpose of the Virgin's apparitions in the first place. The text relates that:

> In the beginning, when the Christian faith had just arrived here in the land . . . the consummate Virgin Saint Mary cherished, aided, and defended the local people so that they might entirely give themselves and adhere to the faith. As a result, they despised and abhorred the idolatry in which they had been wandering about in confusion on the earth. . . . (97)

Through her coming, she desired to "give them her light and aid so that they would recognize the one true deity, God, and through him see and know the heavenly life" (123). She wanted to purify their faith, so that they were no longer bound to the idolatrous worship into which a deceptive demon had lured them. Through her gracious assistance, she sought to redirect their worship to the true God, who alone deserved it.

Laso de la Vega was well aware, though, that the evangelizing enterprise was far from complete, and he looked to Guadalupe as an effective means of propagating and deepening Christian faith in his own day. Hoping both to strengthen new Christians in their faith and to encourage the continued spread of Christianity throughout the region, he sought to circulate the story of her apparition and her miracles. For Laso de la Vega, awareness of Guadalupe was imperative for the spiritual well-being of the Nahuas, and he believed that writing in Nahuatl was the key to ensuring that the Nahuas understand and appropriate the message about Guadalupe.

One can also discern some deeper theological motivations at play in the author's choice to write in Nahuatl. First of all, Laso de la Vega carefully roots his project in the wider Christian tradition. For instance, in his preface he recalls the sign placed on the cross over Jesus' head, which recorded the charge against Jesus in Hebrew (or Aramaic), Latin, and Greek (John 19:20). Drawing on Bonaventure's interpretation of the passage, Laso de la Vega asserts that three languages were used so that "different peoples in different languages would see and marvel at his altogether great and lofty, marvelous love by which he redeemed the peoples of the world through his death on the cross" (57). In the same way, he believes it important that the people in New Spain learn about God's great deed in Guadalupe in their own language. Just as the sign on the cross proclaimed God's redeeming love for the peoples of the world, Laso de la Vega sees himself proclaiming the miracle of Guadalupe that will further the redemption of the inhabitants of the New World.

Moreover, he references Pentecost, highlighting how the descent of the Holy Spirit enabled the disciples to preach about Jesus and his miracles in diverse languages. He especially accentuates the active role of Mary in the Pentecost event, attributing the coming of the Spirit in part to her intercession: "At that time you [Mary] were consoling and encouraging them [the disciples], and also by your petitioning, supplication, and prayer you hastened and summoned the deity, God the Holy Spirit, to come upon them and give himself to them very much for your sake" (59). He then invokes Guadalupe, calling on her to help him imitate this apostolic preaching task through the empowerment of the Spirit. Hoping that he might "receive his [the Holy Spirit's] tongues of fire in order to trace in the Nahuatl language the very great miracle" of Guadalupe, he positions his own project in continuity with biblical examples of God desiring and specially empowering evangelization through the medium of mother tongues.

Laso de la Vega does more than merely appeal to precedent to justify a pragmatic choice in his situation. He implies that reaching out to people in their own language occupies an important place in God's providential plan to evangelize the world. Ultimately, his choice to write in a vernacular language reflects a particular understanding of how God choses to operate in the world. This is a God who wants to make salvation as accessible to humanity as possible. To recognize and respond to this offer, it must be made known to them in their own tongues.

Alongside biblical allusions, Laso de la Vega also justifies his approach with reference to the Guadalupe event itself. He deliberately connects his effort in the manual with the example the Virgin had provided a century earlier, explaining that:

> You have exercised your love in a greater way, when you summoned and called a poor humble commoner in his own language and made a copy of yourself and painted yourself with flowered fragrant hues on his mantle, his maguey cloak, so that he would not mistake you for any other and also so that he would hear and take to heart your utterances and your wishes. And since that is the way you are, I see that you do not spurn the languages of different peoples when you summon them, and thereby you have greatly opened up their hearts. (55)

Throughout the *Nican mopohua* apparition narrative, Guadalupe appears to Juan Diego and Juan Bernardino and addresses them in deeply intimate terms, for instance calling Juan Diego "my youngest child" (65) and assuring him that she holds him "in the security of my lapfold" (79). Further strengthening her identification with the indigenous people, she speaks the local language and imprints herself directly on Juan Diego's *tilma*. Laso de la Vega explicitly characterizes the Virgin's decision to act in this way as an expression of her love for her people.

Laso de la Vega's own choice to write in Nahuatl follows from this consciousness of the Virgin's activity. He likens his effort to make known the miracle of Guadalupe to the way she appeared to Juan Diego and entrusted him with her message and image. The identification is further strengthened when he petitions the Virgin to "receive these humble commoner's words" (55). The ambiguity of the Nahuatl term here could indicate that this is either an expression of "polite self-effacement" or a reference to the use of

Nahuatl itself.[35] In other words, the "humble commoner" could refer to the author himself or to the Nahuas, whose language he used. In either case, it is clear that through his choice to write in Nahuatl, he seeks to imitate the Virgin and express his own love for and devotion to her.

INSIGHTS INTO THE NATURE OF CHRISTIAN FAITH

Laso de la Vega expended great effort to situate his *Huei tlamahuiçoltica* within his particular pastoral context and to respond to some of its challenges. Part of his motivation for promoting devotion to Guadalupe is instrumental: he believes that Guadalupe can serve as a powerful agent of religious change in New Spain. To that end, he presents Guadalupe in a way that makes her as appealing to the Nahuas as possible. She appears to an indigenous man, speaks his language, and singles out the indigenous peoples for her special favor. Moreover, she is an efficacious healer who continues to respond to all who call out to her. But underneath Guadalupe's indigenous face the text presents a piety deeply shaped by European assumptions and devotional traditions. When Laso de la Vega portrays Juan Diego as a model, he does not suggest a radical new way of being Christian. Rather, he depicts a Nahua as capable of embodying an ideal European lay Christian life.

Similarly, as one deeply invested in the effort to colonize and evangelize the peoples of the New World, Laso de la Vega had powerful incentive to downplay the upheaval the indigenous population experienced in the wake of the conquest. He alludes to incidents like epidemics, but he does not recognize the ways in which Christian missionaries and the faith they sought to inculcate were complicit in the disruption the Nahuas underwent. Instead, he presents Christian faith as the unambiguous solution to the pain and difficulties the people face.

Yet even as Laso de la Vega exhibits a Eurocentric orientation, he responds to the situation in seventeenth-century New Spain creatively, and his work contains some profound reflections on the nature of Christian faith. We can only speculate about the degree to which he consciously sought to address these themes, but his pastoral instincts led him to pursue daring theological trajectories. For instance, his portrayal of Guadalupe and her miracles emphasizes the universality of Guadalupe's love and, by extension, God's salvific intent. In the text, she is the mother of all who call

---

35. Sousa et al., *Story of Guadalupe*, 54–55 n 2.

out to her, as is evident in the devotion of both Juan Diego and the bishop, as well as in accounts of miracles performed for Spanish and Nahua suppliants. Moreover, she speaks no words of judgment, even for those who doubt her. Hers is a voice of affirmation that at least hints at the spiritual equality of those of Spanish and Nahua descent, an interpretation validated by the many who have looked to the *Nican mopohua* as a liberating text since its publication.

In portraying the Virgin's unconditional love, Laso de la Vega carefully connects Guadalupe not only with the wider Marian tradition but also with God. He repeatedly links her name and activity with those of "her precious child" (e.g., 115), and he emphasizes her role in bringing people to the true faith and genuine worship of God. Also, the way he frames the text in his introduction associates the story of Guadalupe with God's great deeds and salvific intent in the New Testament. He locates the Guadalupe tradition within the larger stream of salvation history and God's redeeming love.

Laso de la Vega probes the relationship between Christianity and culture throughout his text. Although the piety he portrays is deeply informed by European Marian devotion, his effort to present the Virgin and Marian devotion with an indigenous face is significant. The physical characteristics he assigns Guadalupe, the language she uses, and the Nahuas' responses to her depict grace taking on and operating with an indigenous face. Through Guadalupe, divine grace enters into, speaks, and acts through a particular local cultural context. Reinforcing this impression is Laso de la Vega's aforementioned choice to write in Nahuatl, a decision he connects not only with the Virgin's choice to speak Nahuatl but also with her decision to appear to a commoner and imprint herself on his indigenous cloak. As Lamin Sanneh has pointed out, missionaries' efforts to use the vernacular and cultivate mother-tongue literacy point to deeper theological convictions about the way God works in the world and, in light of that, how the church should evangelize.[36] Indeed, Laso de la Vega's text is rooted in incarnational logic, reflecting commitment to a God who becomes present within ordinary human experience and who communicates divine grace through the mundane.

Jaime Lara observes that although the missionaries in New Spain often successfully engaged in inculturation, they often "alarmed" themselves, for "lacking a sophisticated philosophical/theological concept of inculturation (or even the word *culture*)" they could not distinguish between "pagan

---

36. Sanneh, *Translating the Message*.

survivals" and "authentic Christian 'reinterpretations.'"[37] While this is undoubtedly true, it is important to recognize that the missionaries not only engaged in inculturation in practice but also sought to formulate theoretical support for doing so. While Laso de la Vega was far from articulating a full-fledged theology of inculturation, he took some important steps in that direction. Based on his own pastoral experience and that of the missionaries who had worked in New Spain before him, he began to reflect on the relationship of his Christian faith to particular cultural expressions. He put those concepts into practice in his pastoral manual, and he used both the Christian tradition and the experience of the Guadalupe event to justify doing so. Here, as elsewhere, missionary vernacular efforts constitute a core element of a wider project of inculturation.

Throughout the text, Laso de la Vega emphasized the transformative dimension of the Guadalupe event, and he believed that an encounter with Guadalupe could help transform the Nahuas into good Christians. Indeed, we can detect the Virgin's transformative capacity in Laso de la Vega's own life, for reflecting on the Guadalupe event in light of the challenges of his pastoral context led him to probe the way God's salvific love transcends the boundaries of social or cultural location.

BIBLIOGRAPHY

de Berceo, Gonzalo. *The Miracles of Our Lady (Milagros de Nuestra Señora)*. Translated by Richard Terry Mount and Annette Grant Cash. Lexington: University Press of Kentucky, 1997.

Brading, D. A. *Mexican Phoenix: Our Lady of Guadalupe; Image and Tradition across Five Centuries*. Cambridge: Cambridge University Press, 2001.

Burkhart, Louise M. *The Slippery Earth: Nahua-Christian Moral Dialogue in Sixteenth-Century Mexico*. Tucson: University of Arizona Press, 1989.

Elizondo, Virgilio. *Guadalupe: Mother of the New Creation*. Maryknoll, NY: Orbis, 1997.

Heath, Shirley Brice. *Telling Tongues: Language Policy in Mexico, Colony to Nation*. New York and London: Teachers College Press, 1972.

Lafaye, Jacques. *Quetzalcóatl and Guadalupe: The Formation of Mexican National Consciousness, 1531–1813*. Translated by Benjamin Keen. Chicago: University of Chicago Press, 1976.

Lara, Jaime. *Christian Texts for Aztecs: Art and Liturgy in Colonial Mexico*. Notre Dame, IN: University of Notre Dame Press, 2008.

---

37. Lara, *Christian Texts*, 255, 257.

Matovina, Timothy. "The First Guadalupan Pastoral Manual: Luis Laso de la Vega's *Huei tlamahuiçoltica* (1649)." *Horizons: The Journal of the College Theology Society* 40 (2013) 159–77.

Pardo, Osvaldo F. *The Origins of Mexican Catholicism: Nahua Rituals and Christian Sacraments in Sixteenth-Century Mexico.* Ann Arbor: University of Michigan Press, 2004.

Ricard, Robert. *The Spiritual Conquest of Mexico: An Essay on the Apostolate and the Evangelizing Methods of the Mendicant Orders in New Spain, 1523–1572.* Translated by Lesley Byrd Simpson. Berkeley: University of California Press, 1966.

Sanneh, Lamin. *Translating the Message: The Missionary Impact on Culture.* Maryknoll, NY: Orbis, 1989.

Sousa, Lisa, Stafford Poole, and James Lockhart, eds. and trans. *The Story of Guadalupe: Luis Laso de la Vega's* Huei tlamahuiçoltica *of 1649.* Stanford: Stanford University Press, 1998.

Trexler, Richard C. "From the Mouths of Babes: Christianization by Children in Sixteenth-Century New Spain." In *Church and Community, 1200–1600: Studies in the History of Florence and New Spain*, 549–73. Rome: Edizioni di storia e letteratura, 1987.

———. "We Think, They Act: Clerical Readings of Missionary Theatre in Sixteenth-Century Mexico." In *Church and Community, 1200–1600: Studies in the History of Florence and New Spain*, 575–613. Rome: Edizioni di storia e letteratura, 1987.

5

Mother of Health, Remedy for the Plague

Preaching on Guadalupe in the Midst of Death

Michael Griffin

THE PLAGUE. It is a word with ubiquitous historical application. In the Bible, the Ten Plagues—described in graphic detail in the book of Exodus—spell the end of Pharaoh's rule, along with destruction for countless Egyptians. Other ancient civilizations waged classic and often losing struggles with various plagues, which were experienced as a kind of apocalyptic blow to the collective life. Historically, the term *plague* often conjures for us images of the great menace of European history: the bubonic plague, or Black Death. But even in contemporary times and places where public health is not so fragile, the idea of the plague is never far from minds and lips. Certainly epidemics such as HIV/AIDS are modern plagues, but we also use the term to refer to ominous events that we should avoid "like the plague." Clearly, the term has implications that go to the heart of shared life: across many epochs and many cultures, people have been forced to deal with plagues that threaten the common good. Thus, the ways in which people have chosen to fight or not fight them provides a privileged set of glimpses into human nature.

Perhaps the best-known scholar to study the social context of plagues is René Girard, who repeatedly takes up the question of what plagues are and how societies have dealt with them. In his book *I See Satan Fall Like*

mother of health, remedy for the plague

Lightning, Girard states clearly his thesis that "the plague" is a kind of social disorder—sometimes with epidemiological symptoms, other times displayed through violent enmity or turmoil—and that the classic response to plagues involves reestablishing social cohesion. For Girard, of course, humanity has found no better means of social cohesion than ritual sacrifice. He eschews a perspective on ancient sacrificial violence that sees it as just part of "irrational religious systems" and claims instead that:

> according to the peoples directly involved, and *perhaps it is time to listen to what they believed*, sacrifices were intended (1) to please the gods, who had prescribed them to the community, and (2) to consolidate or restore, if need be, the order and peace of the community.[1]

Particularly extensive is one account Girard gives of "The Horrible Miracle of Apollonius of Tyana,"[2] which recounts the healing of "a plague epidemic in the city of Ephesus" in the second century CE by means of a ritual stoning of a beggar who is brought into an amphitheater filled with angry citizens. Apollonius unites the crowd into the decision to lay blame on the man and to stone him, which they do and which becomes the ritual credited with ending the plague. The stoned man in Ephesus reminds Girard of the Greek *pharmakoi*, who were paraded through the streets of Athens, beaten, expelled and sometimes killed in order to provide the remedy (*pharmakon*) for a plague. What is fascinating about Girard's analysis is that over against the usual understanding of plague as a medical, physical spread of disease, he points out that plagues can also be seen as social crises of mimetic rivalry which has snowballed into a "contagion." In this light, the creation of a common enemy against which the community can form a violent and cohesive coalition is precisely an effective remedy to "the plague."

My intention here is not to elaborate, much less adjudicate, such a sophisticated and totalizing theory as Girard's. However, I do believe his perspective on plagues raises some important questions for scholars, historians in particular, and most especially for theologians trying to understand how *religious* ritual has played a role in resolving social pathologies of all kinds.

For Christian theologians, of course, the obvious question would be whether there is violence, hidden or overt, in the attempts of our own

---

1. Girard, *I See Satan Fall*, 78. Emphasis mine.
2. Ibid., 49–61.

religious tradition to bring the unity and social cohesion necessary to restore peace. Girard would surely admit such violence, but his claim is that the message of the Gospels is precisely that Christianity unleashes a kind of *anti-sacrificial contagion* which can bring peace without scapegoating—precisely because Jesus on the Cross "unveils" the truth about ritual violence and the risen Christ "exposes" it as a failure. In its place, the Lord offers peace, though not as the world offers it (John 14:27). For the theologian attentive to history, the task thus becomes to locate instances of the plague in which Christianity is able to help resolve the crisis *without* the time-honored instrument of some sort of sacrificial scapegoating. I will present in this essay one such instance, though the larger context of pre- and post-conquest Mexico certainly bears the marks of a society permeated by the constant turn to sacrificial violence—be it of the Aztec or Spanish variety—in order to "restore" the social order.

CONTENDING WITH THE MATLAZAHUATL

In December of 1736, an ominous revelation descended upon the inhabitants of Mexico City: a plague was among them. They called it *matlazahuatl*—an epidemic of typhus, or typhoid fever. This was by no means the first public health menace to face their post-conquest world. In 1576 a similar outbreak of the disease—which spreads in conditions of poor sanitation when the *Salmonella typhi* bacteria get into food or water—decimated the city and lived long in the collective memory of the people. The losing battle with that epidemic was a factor in the early flurry of activities and strategies to tackle the new *matlazahuatl* directly. Indeed, the diversity of mechanisms employed is one theme in the story of this battle: between December 1736 and May 1737, a wide array of what we today would call "sacred" and "secular" powers were placed at the service of saving human lives from the deadly disease.[3] A brief summary serves to display the depth of the crisis felt by the inhabitants and the breadth of the measures taken:

- The image of Our Lady of Loretto, brought from Italy by Jesuits, was paraded through the streets of the city in December 1736, and enshrined in the Jesuit church for supplication.

---

3. Cf. Brading, *Mexican Phoenix*, 120–25.

mother of health, remedy for the plague

- Three religious orders established special hospital units to care for the sick and dying. The Jesuits also added an outreach program to poor houses from which patients were unable to leave.
- The prodigious Spanish devotion to Our Lady of Los Remedios was invoked for aid in January 1737, and she was installed on the high altar of the Cathedral of Mexico City.
- Also early in 1737, a series of medical dispensaries, funded by Archbishop Juan Antonio de Vizarrón y Eguiarreta, were operational, along with a pastoral plan by which diocesan priests ministered to the sick.
- By March, a panoply of sacred images were invoked, including many images of Christ—especially images of the *Ecce homo* variety which display his Passion. These measures came to a dramatic conclusion in April when the holy image of the Crucified Christ of Ixmiquilpan was brought out and processed through the streets by the clergy and into the Cathedral as the bells tolled the *Miserere*.
- Processions at this time also included many popular saints. Perhaps most interestingly, Santiago loomed large in lay-led pilgrimages, with his image altered: in place of his traditional sword he wielded a scourge, and rather than the clothing of a warrior he wore the garb of a penitent.[4]

Of all the many responses to the *matlazahuatl* in the early months of 1737, however, none was more common or cohesive than appeals to Our Lady of Guadalupe. It might be convenient to narrate the invocation of Guadalupe as a case of "bringing out the big gun" after all other attempts had failed. Yet the truth is that the turn to her was early—and emerged from what might seem to us an interesting source. In January 1737, the City Council sought to bring the image of Guadalupe to the Mexico City Cathedral. Archbishop Vizarrón responded that instead, the people should *go to her*, at Tepeyac. Thus, the story is not one in which after all the secular measures were tried and failed, the religious authorities invoked sacred power. Rather, from the beginning, Guadalupe had popular support as one element in the multi-pronged strategy to face down the *matlazahuatl*. Moreover, it is clear that after the City Council's initiative and dialogue with the archbishop in January, events moved quickly. In February, a great procession to

---

4. All of the historical information in this section comes from Brading's summary in *Mexican Phoenix*, 123–24.

Tepeyac was staged. By the end of March the City Council had decided to request that "Our Lady the most Holy Virgin in her admirable, miraculous Image of Guadalupe" be named principal patron of the city.[5] In April this was granted and in May it was celebrated with a parade—attended heavily by indigenous, *criollo* and Spaniards alike—carrying a life-size silver statue of the *Guadalupana* through the streets.

What was the practical result? In one sense, all the measures failed to avert a disaster: in the city alone at least forty thousand died and in the entire region the figure reached upwards of two hundred thousand.[6] And yet, as the intensification of devotion from March to May suggests, a sense arose that perhaps the *matlazahuatl* was yielding to divine intercession. Indeed, by June the plague was in decline and it became clear to all that a potentially far worse calamity had been averted. The only question—as relevant to the many actors then as it would be to epidemiologists today—was which of the many measures were most effective and how were they related to one another? Of course, we are unable to have access to a sufficiently sophisticated set of health data to make a scientific examination. Indeed, the properly scientific response would hypothesize that precisely no effect came directly from the intervention of Saints, the Blessed Mother or Jesus Christ himself. That leaves open the question, even for the scientist, of an indirect role for the power of supplication—perhaps one in which devotions provided the needed penitential stance or sense of solidarity—in defeating the epidemic. Another kind of analysis might take a Girardian perspective, searching for hidden signs of scapegoating or sacrificial expulsion or, on the contrary, signs of a Christian cohesion built on concern for the victim. In any case, each of these lines of interpretation runs a conspicuous risk of anachronism in dividing and analyzing discrete measures like so many pieces of a modernist puzzle. Thus, far more important than how *we* might assess the panoply of actors and outcomes in 1737 is how *they* understood the events happening in their midst. Again, no comprehensive analysis is possible here, since the sources are so few. However, we do have access to two primary documents: a sermon from the midst of the *matlazahuatl* in 1737 and a book from 1746 which in part offers a more ponderous look at the larger meaning of the momentous events which took place during the plague. The book, *Escudo de Armas de Mexico* by Cayetano de Cabrera y Quintero, is well known and the main reference point for what scholarly

5. Ibid., 125.
6. Ibid., 120.

work there is on the epidemic. The sermon, however, has received much less attention, and thus will become the focus of my analysis for the ways in which it brings to light a fresh perspective on Guadalupe which in its origin was central to her rise in stature among the Mexican people.

ITA Y PARRA INVOKES GUADALUPE AS THE MOTHER OF HEALTH

The response of the archbishop to the City Council's request to bring Guadalupe to the city center, namely *that the people rather should go to her*, underscored the need for proper homage to the local Virgin. Thus the pilgrimage to her included a novena, culminating in a final invocation of Guadalupe as the key to restoration of health. That invocation came in the form of the sermon at the ninth day Mass, on February 7, 1737, preached by Padre Bartolomé Felipe de Ita y Parra, the renowned homilist of many important occasions, including the bicentennial of the apparition. The homily of Ita y Parra was titled "La Madre de la Salud" (The Mother of Health) and provides a valuable, firsthand account of the kind of aid being sought from Guadalupe and, more precisely, the kind of devotion being prescribed as medicine for the people. What follows is my analysis of this text[7], which will serve to provide a sense of the relevant themes and theological claims in this important source.

At the beginning of his homily, Ita y Parra marks clearly the social context: "the pitiful epidemic we suffer."[8] He also places the events of the moment within the whole sweep of salvation history, beginning when humanity "was infected to death in Adam" and culminating in Christ who is "the owner and Lord of health" and who came "healing all of us from that common lethal disease." Only after he establishes the wider context does Ita y Parra move to "the particular" and seek the aid of the "magnificent image of Guadalupe" who represents Mary, the "Mother of our desired health in the current contagion."[9]

---

7. I was assisted in this task by Carmina Colorado, student at Holy Cross College and Notre Dame's Instituto Cultural de Liderazgo en Medio Oeste program, and María Elena Bessignano of Notre Dame's Institute for Latino Studies.

8. *Siete Sermones Guadalupanos*, 85–106, Paragraph 1. Hereafter I will use only the paragraph number for the references, since that is how the homily was originally published. The full title of the sermon was "La Madre de la Salud, La Milagrosa Imagen de Guadalupe."

9. Ibid., 3.

The fact that Ita y Parra situates the current moment on the canvass of salvation history is important for at least two reasons. First, it makes clear that the rationale for supplication to this and other images during the plague should not be put at odds with basic Christian theological claims. There is no doubt who the Lord of history is and the fact that his power alone can heal and save. Second, the sermon's movement toward the particular affliction threatening Mexico is narrated in a way parallel to the particularized stories of Scripture. That is, just as the biblical authors' presentation of a rich symbolic world to narrate events does not diminish the role of the main protagonist, God, so too with Ita y Parra: he scans the present landscape for particular symbols in a way that does not detract from the larger story being told about God's love for this people. The best example of this is the way he introduces the symbolic value of the Guadalupan image itself: he compares it to the burning bush (*la zarza*) of Exodus. He then plays with this imagery at length, but never reifying the symbol, as if *la imagen* or *la zarza* is the source of power. Rather, the symbolism allows him to say something about the deeper connection of God to the suffering supplicants.

GUADALUPE AND THE BURNING BUSH

This connection is made clear in the way Ita y Parra introduces the *zarza* motif. He refers first to the "testament's Ark," the stone that was hewn by Moses and then brought to Sinai for the Lord to inscribe the Commandments. This symbol, which indeed, will bear the divine message, is like a powerful image of Our Lady of Los Remedios. But more than the stone tablets, *la zarza* is a symbol for the gratuitous inbreaking and unmerited visitation of the divine presence on local soil. Thus, while Remedios, "brought it from Europe," is a symbol of the abiding presence of the Lord in the journeys of his people, Guadalupe "was born here: here, she appears in this place: and she chooses this territory."[10] And for this reason, while Remedios has been brought "to Mexico"—most recently in the January processions—the reverse is now true: "Mexico comes to Guadalupe," just as Moses approached the burning bush.[11] Of course, quite evident here is the perennial contest between the two great Marian devotions of that time and place, which I will analyze below. But what is more germane to the

10. Ibid., 7.
11. Ibid.

context of the plague is the way in which Ita y Parra connects the symbols of Guadalupe/*la zarza* to the themes of God's love and, more precisely, to the cause for hope in the midst of the plague.

An interesting entry point to the arena of symbolic meaning in the sermon is the simple question: Why did Ita y Parra choose the burning bush, of all the images available, to invoke the aid of Guadalupe? The text itself offers clear reasons, rooted in the social context of the plague, but first I wish to mention a reason that the preacher does not mention but which was offered by Carmina Colorado, who assisted my translation of the text. A basic feature of the Exodus text is that God is speaking from within nature. By no means is this unique to the story, but it is among the first and most explicit instances of the phenomenon. Similar to this particular example of "botanical revelation" is the generalized element in the Aztec thought and symbol world by which a primary means of divine communication is flowers. *Flor*. Indeed, from the most scholarly interpreter of Guadalupe to the most grassroots, all can see the importance of "botanical revelation" in the story. Thus we might ask whether Ita y Parra chooses to focus on *la zarza* because of the way that the narrative of Guadalupe "trained" him to be aware of this symbolic element. More importantly, do *la zarza* and *La Guadalupana* create for him two bookends of salvation history that give evidence of the hopeful fact that God is still speaking? There are other explanatory options. Perhaps Ita y Parra uses the holy ground of the burning bush—which is approached and does not approach—to defend the archbishop's decision that the image of Guadalupe cannot travel to the city, but must be visited. Of course, Ita y Parra does not provide us an answer as to his motives, but he does explain why the burning bush and Guadalupe are closely connected narratives.

The explicit reason offered by Ita y Parra for invoking the burning bush is a different aspect of the symbolism which emerged in 1531 at Tepeyac: there appeared Guadalupe "embraced by fire" so that she herself became "a source of light."[12] And yet despite the intense, burning heat of the sun which surrounded her, she was unharmed like the "the Zarza, which remains in its entirety."[13] More to the present point, the Virgin was not only tranquil in the midst of intense heat, but even in the face "of two passing centuries" and the "insatiable voracity" of the *matlazahuatl*, we are still

---

12. Ibid., 9.
13. Ibid.

able to "miraculously venerate the ayate [tilma] in its entirety."[14] Portraying Guadalupe as the burning bush thus allows Ita y Parra to place the puzzling juxtaposition of destructive force and abiding presence within a context of hope. This theme will reemerge: the plague may claim our city and it may claim our neighbors and it may claim us, but Guadalupe will remain unscathed, a sign of God's enduring presence and that we, like Moses, walk on holy ground.

The image of *la zarza* did not, however, signify only sweetness and light. Ita y Parra also presents the dark side of the symbolism, focusing on the *thorns* of the burning bush. The need to deal with these thorns provides a natural reason why the bush needed to be visited by the "law-abiding God," whose fire punishes evil.[15] Ita y Parra specifies the evildoers, quoting St. Peter Chrysologus: "the thorns represented those sinners and ingrates among the Hebrews."[16] In this metaphor, the fire is designed to "destroy" the thorns/sinners, but Ita y Parra actually shifts the imagery in three subtle moves. First, he clarifies that what God intends to destroy are "our offenses"; the point is not to destroy people, but sin.[17] Secondly, following Theodoto—an early church, possibly Gnostic source upon whom Ita y Parra draws heavily here—he subtly moves away from the claim that in the fire/heat God "punishes" and instead uses the verb "purify" to describe the action on the bush. The preference for purification language allows Ita y Parra to claim that pain—past or present, symbolic or real—is for the sake of the common good, not mere retribution. But a third, more radical move, is then made in the sermon which qualifies even more his theological interpretation of the present suffering. In short, he claims that on the burning bush who is Guadalupe, God spares even the thorns! Since this claim will emerge as central to understanding the sermon's message to those suffering the plague, it is important to examine more closely this move of Ita y Parra.

GUADALUPE'S SPECIAL PROTECTION

Ita y Parra prepares the assembly to ponder the divine act of mercy toward the "thorns" by setting the stage in which God comes down to the midst of evildoers, "The strict judge is among the prisoners; the law-abiding God

14. Ibid.
15. Ibid., 10.
16. Ibid.
17. Ibid.

mother of health, remedy for the plague

is in those prisoners' thorns. He keeps them close for their punishment."[18] And so with justice calling for destruction and the divine fire ready to consume them, could it be that "they are not afraid?"[19] Indeed, they are not, and the reason: roses. Roses not only, as one might expect, make the whole bush worth saving, but also take away the repugnance of the thorns. And here Ita y Parra moves explicitly to the Guadalupe story to explain that it is Mary who is the rose among thorns and who tempers the avenging fire of God: "she soothes His fury with her beauty."[20]

At this point Ita y Parra is at his most theological: the reason why the law-abiding God will not destroy sinners is because it was in the womb of Mary that God "humanized."[21] This union of God and humanity through Mary creates a bond of beneficence as it were, such that God "does not punish them but purifies them; does not consume them but benefits them."[22] In this way, far from being a thorny thicket of sin, the bush symbolizes that the Virgin has healing power. Here he quotes St. Ambrose: "That Zarza had virtue in its leaves to kill serpents."[23] In the present context, the most dangerous serpent to be killed is the *matlazahuatl* and the virtue of clinging of Guadalupe has the power to do just that. We must remember, though, that central to this claim is that the bond of beneficence is through Mary. Thus, Ita y Parra is not describing a general amnesty from punishment, but rather is delimiting a penumbra of protection in which the people can have confidence. The theme of a special space free of punishment and destruction migrates from the biblical text into the dark heart of the *matlazahuatl* in what is Ita y Parra's most direct treatment of the actual conditions of the plague. He begins this migration by noting that divine favor is granted not because of the virtue of Mexico, whose sins are like those of Babylon. But unlike Babylon, Tepeyac has the "sovereign image" which "calms God's fury" and which is thus "Mother of our health in the current contagion" because through her God "grants us life."[24] And Ita y Parra means health and life quite literally here. In undoubtedly the most striking observation

18. Ibid., 11.
19. Ibid.
20. Ibid.
21. Ibid.
22. Ibid.
23. Ibid., 9.
24. Ibid., 13.

of the entire sermon, which deserves to be quoted in full, he notes of the regions surrounding Tepeyac:

> Surrounding villages are infested by all four winds with the contagion, some almost devastated; in Guadalupe's enclosure, there is not a single ill person! Oh shock! Astonishing! The wonderful miracle of that canvas (tilma) is extraordinary, prodigious.[25]

In trying to contextualize such a startling occurrence as the lack of anyone suffering—let alone dying—from the *matlazahuatl* in the region of Tepeyac, Ita y Parra can only be satisfied with an allusion to the plagues of Egypt, which afflicted the people of Pharaoh and left unscathed the Israelites. Now, we are correct to at least question the historical claim here about the lack of epidemic in Tepeyac proper. Is he defining "the enclosure" of Guadalupe simply to mean the temple itself? And even if that included a rectory or convent, it would still be a dubious rationale for a miracle—akin perhaps to using the patronage of St. Peter to explain why no one in the Vatican has died of hunger. But the absence of epidemiological data also means that we cannot dismiss the claim here, and Ita y Parra goes on to suggest that he is not playing fast and loose with the "enclosure," that he is referring to an actual inhabited region that otherwise would be suffering the *matlazahuatl* but is not, and that there is historical precedent for Guadalupe's special role as mother of health. He refers to the year 1544, when "a plague ignited among the Indians" that within a few days killed 12,000 people. In response, the Indians took to the streets and processed to "this Sacred Image, at that point the contagion ceased."[26]

THE UNCEASING MANANTIAL: GUADALUPE AS MEDICINE

Whether the 1544 incident or the claim about Tepeyac enjoying special protection from the 1737 plague is historically accurate is not essential to analyzing the method and message of this sermon (though, as noted, Cabrera y Quintero would later identify the alleviation of the epidemic as coinciding with the successful campaign to make Guadalupe patron). What, then, is the importance of Ita y Parra placing safety—and not just spiritual safety—within the mantle of Guadalupe? The answer comes in the

25. Ibid., 19
26. Ibid.

mother of health, remedy for the plague

way that he narrates the apparition account itself. The first and only time in the sermon that the "blessed and beloved Indian Juan Diego" is explicitly invoked is to recall the words of the Virgin to him in her first appearance. After calling Juan her son and identifying herself as the mother of the true God, Guadalupe makes a direct request of Juan: "my wish is that in this place a temple be built, here, I will show myself as a merciful Mother to you and yours; with my devotees and those others who seek my help to remedy their necessities."[27] What is critical here is the specification of who will receive her assistance, namely those tied to her by location—the Indians, "the ones like Juan"—and those others devoted to her. Interestingly, Ita y Parra here seems to be using the briefer, direct text of Miguel Sánchez rather than the *Nican mopohua* translation of Laso de Vega, which allows for a more expansive construal of who will receive the assistance.[28] This brings into sharp focus that for Ita y Parra, the ones to be protected are the ones who, as he puts it, "come here."[29]

Precisely as this point of specification, the image of the sermon shifts from Guadalupe as the burning bush to Guadalupe as a spring, flowing abundantly with "the healing waters." The one who is able to "take a bath" will experience health and life—of the body and soul.[30] Ita y Parra does not exclude the idea of Guadalupan spring, which flows "non-stop," symbolizes a maternal and medicinal affection that moves beyond geography, but he is at pains to identify these healings waters with her sanctuary. One reason, which comes out clearly in the closing of the sermon, is that her "place" is among "the Indians, the sick and special children of Guadalupe, who belong to that particular loving jurisdiction."[31] A striking element of this claim is the implicit recognition that the Indians were at special risk in the *matlazahuatl* due to lack of resources, and yet in this dangerous region is found the jurisdiction of La Virgen and the most clear offer of medicinal love. In fact, perhaps the most tender moment of the sermon comes when Ita y Parra narrates the Virgin speaking a special word not just to all those in attendance

---

27. Ibid., 16. Emphasis mine.
28. The relevant translation of Sánchez and Laso de le Vega was found in Brading, *Mexican Phoenix*, 24, against which I checked the Ita y Parra sermon.
29. *Siete Sermones Guadalupanos*, 18.
30. Ibid.
31. Ibid., 29.

but in particular to those in "despair": "If the contagion and fear of death upsets you, come to me; because in me, for sure, is all hope of life."[32]

GUADALUPE AND REMEDIOS: RIVALS OR COLLABORATORS?

If the message of Guadalupe to the suffering people of Mexico is "come to me," then the question arises why so many civic leaders have turned to other images, most notably Our Lady of Los Remedios. Ita y Parra begins by noting that the reason Remedios first visit invoked by the Spanish governor was to solicit "means and measures," practical necessities like food, medicine and new hospitals which required "numerous alms" in order to battle effectively this "stubborn epidemic."[33] But these efforts did not seem to deter the plague. At this point in the sermon—especially after the *arca/zarza* dichotomy—the assembly might be anticipating that the preacher will drive a final nail in the coffin of Remedios devotion and pronounce Guadalupe the sole Virgin worthy of supplication.

Ita y Parra does not make this move. Nor does he move to diminish the importance of practical efforts to fight the plague, such as those the governor sought under the patronage of Remedios. Instead, he lays out a rather complicated process by which Remedios and Guadalupe are working in collaboration, such that the former "brings us the image" in order to bring about a full restoration of health.[34] The basic premise here is that "both images have the same power, because it is the same Lady."[35] But in her guise as Remedios, rooted in Spanish tradition, Mary understands that this region of the Indians is not her proper home, not her jurisdiction, and so she leads the people to their own Virgin, Guadalupe, for assistance. What repeatedly captivates Ita y Parra in this strategy is its secrecy: "whereas in private the image of Remedios heals us, in public the image of Guadalupe give us health."[36] He even recounts at length the story in the Gospel where Jesus heals a leper, then "asked him to keep it to himself" and instructs him to go and offer thanks to the priest, who has Mosaic authority over events

32. Ibid., 18.
33. Ibid., 20
34. Ibid., 21.
35. Ibid., 27.
36. Ibid., 21.

of this nature and who is to be, in any case, "the image of Jesus Christ."[37] The use of this story is instructive in the way Ita y Parra uses the concepts of jurisdiction and image to explain the secret work of God. Here, and elsewhere, the sermon is not concerned with direct causality and precision—in this exegesis, a Levitical priest is invoked as the image of Jesus—but rather the portrait presented is a kind of symphony of collaboration, and the Remedios-Guadalupe relationship is the example *par excellence*.

Ita y Parra turns to the story of Ruth and Naomi to explain the relationship further: Ruth, like Remedios, is a visitor to a new land, and so pledges to her host: "where you go, I will go" and (in the succinct Latin the sermon invokes here) "*populus tuus, populus meus*." (Ruth 1:16) But he also uses the story of the Indian Cacique Don Juan as an example of the kind of collaboration at work in New Spain. Don Juan had the image of Los Remedios in his house, but he took the image and enshrined it publicly in an outside *hermita*. For this "God punished him with a dangerous illness" that would certainly mean death.[38] Desperately ill, Don Juan asked to be taken to the image of Guadalupe, where he repented and asked for his health. "I grant it to you," responded the image, and he left "well and healed."[39] No doubt, this story was easily used by others in a narrative of rivalry and Guadalupan victory, but Ita y Parra employs it for the opposite effect. Don Juan's original enshrinement of the statue was not just offensive to Guadalupe, but to Remedios herself, who never "declared her will" desiring the hermitage—and indeed she would not have, being a pilgrim image outside her jurisdiction.[40]

Theologically, Ita y Parra is aware that positing such a divine scheme of collaborating images requires a defense that does not reify the objects of devotions as if they are gods. And he provides such a defense. After admitting that it would seem he is daring to guess the secrets of Mary, he instead roots himself again on the solid ground of tradition: "based on the teachings of San Pablo, invisible things such as God are known through the visible . . . the hidden mysteries of Providence can be tracked by its facts."[41] Thus he is aware that the plentiful use of symbols, metaphors and images does not fully capture the hidden mysteries of Providence. It is true that his

37. Ibid., 28.
38. Ibid., 23.
39. Ibid.
40. Ibid., 24.
41. Ibid., 22.

citation of Paul suggests that the invisible truths "are known" via the visible world, but his Spanish verb here, *se rastrean*, is more telling, connoting not so much knowing as tracing, searching, fathoming. The stories and symbols of Scripture and tradition give powerful insight into God's presence, but ultimately are only clues to a love that moves in secret. Thus, faced with the temptation to make devotion to sacred images the direct-line mechanism by which the plague will or will not be defeated, Ita y Parra opts for a more humble stance. And faced with a temptation perhaps stronger still, to present a narrative of dueling devotions in which a victor is declared, Ita y Parra offers a paradigm of collaboration.

ITA Y PARRA IN A GIRARDIAN KEY

The closing words of the homily strike a theme that brings us back to the introduction of this essay and the theory of René Girard about how plagues are usually resolved: through *sacrifice*. In preaching this theme, Ita y Parra once again retrieves a biblical narrative, in this case invoking in brief the story from 1 Chronicles of the way in which King David deals with a deadly plague threatening to destroy Jerusalem (cf. 1 Chr 21). In his telling of the climactic decision, Ita y Parra emphasizes that David took the advice of his prophet Gad and erected a new altar in the land of the Jebusites so that "in there, he would offer sacrifices to God; which would calm God's fury and cease the plague."[42] We see here clear resonance with the ancient idea that sacrifice placates God and restores social unity. But once again, Ita y Parra makes some surprising moves with the symbolism. Noting that the site for David's altar had been beloved by God, but certainly "not more than this" site of Guadalupe, he hails the *new* kind of sacrifice which is offered at Tepeyac. And he closes the entire sermon by repeating one final time that it is the Indians who will receive the benefits of the "new cults" "in that place," specifically "abundance in their grains, fertility in their fields, prosperity in their times, medicine in their illnesses, health in their living, grace in their souls, and glory in Eternity."[43]

Though he specifies the beneficiaries of the "new cults," Ita y Parra ends the sermon without giving us a clear picture of what kind of sacrifice is involved. He provides some indication in the lead-up to his conclusion, where he envisions the day in Mexico when the hopes of "both domains,

42. Ibid., 31.
43. Ibid.

Ecclesiastical and Secular" are realized to have Guadalupe as their patron.[44] On that day, there will be "a festive atmosphere on earth" and "all its nations" will be able to "consecrate cults."[45] Here "cults" seems to refer to particular expressions and organizations of devotion in accord with local customs. Indeed this kind of unity and common good was the very reason that "in this place our Lady wanted to come to us, in that unique Image, to connect to her all of New Spain's prosperity."[46] Thus we can begin to see a picture emerge in which the social cohesion achieved through the sacrifice of devotion to Guadalupe is quite different from rituals in which there is a victim. Moreover, in each of the already presented themes of the sermon there are hints of what Girard might call a victimless, or non-sacrificial resolution to social crises. Guadalupe becomes a key in adopting solidarity, rather than scapegoating, as the response to the *matlazahuatl* plague. To make this point fully, I must go beyond a strict analysis of Ita y Parra's theology and put his homily in conversation with my own theological voice, as well as concepts drawn from Girard. But this task, coming after a close analysis of what Ita y Parra actually preached, is consistent with his approach: a creative employment of traditional sources to construct a new narrative that speaks to the contemporary situation. With this caveat stated, I will claim the latitude to theologize briefly about each of the sermon's four themes, concluding with one suggestion about the general relevance of Guadalupan devotion for the current crisis plaguing Mexico.

Guadalupe as the Burning Bush

The emphasis that Ita y Parra places on the burning heat that surrounds *la zarza*, as well as Guadalupe, makes clear the same message offered in the book of Exodus: God is with us, even in the midst of suffering. The maternal stability of Mary offers hope to those suffering just as the strength of a mom comforts a sick or struggling child: it is not simply what she does *for you*, but her *example* as one able to withstand the heat of life. Ita y Parra, as mentioned, plays quite liberally with the imagery of the thorns of the bush, even suggesting at first their symbolism as the ingrate sinners of Israel whom God will burn with his punishing fire. But he rejects this trajectory and opts instead for a symbol system in which Guadalupe, the

44. Ibid., 30.
45. Ibid.
46. Ibid.

"rose amid thorns" renders the whole bush protected. And yet hidden in his sermon was that one word suggestion of what it was that won God's favor for the whole bush: beauty. It was Mary's beauty that was decisive; "she soothes His fury with her beauty." Here we can see the Girardian theme of placation come to the fore. Whereas the ancient form of placation was through sacrificing a victim who is offered to God, here what is offered to God is beauty. It is not a scapegoat that calms the divine fury, though such a mechanism is often thought to describe even the sacrifice of Christ on the Cross. For Girard, what the crucified Christ offers to the Father is a kind of beauty, a love that stays faithful to the end. This kind of sacrifice pleases God, as seems to be the insight of the Psalmist, "in sacrifice I take no delight; my sacrifice is a contrite spirit" (Ps 51) as well as Dostoevsky in the famous maxim that "beauty saves the world."[47] Thus, the beauty of Guadalupe—and, I might add, devotion to her—has a kind of power which is able to overcome the intense heat of life, or at least make life more bearable, more human, more beautiful in the midst of it.

Guadalupe's Special Protection

No doubt the most interesting claim of Ita y Parra's sermon is that around the shrine of Guadalupe existed a kind of "safe zone" from the plague. I already mentioned that questions about the historical or epidemiological validity of this claim are not essential to understanding the theological point of the sermon. But let us suppose for a moment that the claim is true; of course the question would become, *why is it true?* What if we were to imagine that the zone of protection were the result not of the magical sense of miracle, but of the sense of human solidarity that comes with taking seriously membership in God's family? That is, we might imagine that at this holy place a deep sense of reverence is cultivated not only for God but for human life, and consequently the environment has protective elements of care not cultivated in other places. Such a view would not collapse divine protection into a constructed program of public health; rather divine and human agency would mingle to create a community in which human life truly is sacred. Moreover, Ita y Parra's claim is part of a larger genre in Christian tradition by which a place of apparition and/or pilgrimage is said to have been spared the destructive effects of a calamity.[48] Indeed, this

---

47. From his novel *The Idiot*, attributed to Prince Myskin.
48. The most recent of such claims comes from Medjugorje, which devotees claim

vision of a protected community also accords with ancient understandings of monasteries—not as a protective enclosure from worldly risk but rather as a kind of community of physical and spiritual health that can be an exemplar of what is possible for human society.

The Unceasing Manantial: Guadalupe as Medicine

One of the clearest conclusions about the Gospel accounts of healing is that, as Jesus affirms repeatedly, faith saves. The medicinal effect of faith, of course, can make it into a dangerous opiate if the expectation is that God will spare from suffering those who believe. As history shows, quite the opposite is often true. And yet Jesus says to people healed in spirit and in body: your faith has saved you. Thus, when Ita y Parra describes Guadalupe as a spring, flowing with the medicinal waters of true life, we ought to understand this claim in its Christian light, that she leads pilgrims to faith in Christ. This faith, in turn, has the power to free us—most especially from fear, as we also see repeatedly in the Gospel. And the sermon includes precisely this point, if only in one phrase where a special appeal is made to those living in "fear of death"[49] As explained, Ita y Parra explicitly acknowledges that those with most to fear are the Indians, suffering as they did the brunt of the *matlazahuatl*. Notice here that the medicine of Guadalupe is offered precisely and firstly to them, the marginalized: how different than our usual public health system! And how different from the social mechanisms of ancient Greece, detailed by Girard. In that culture the "medicine" (*pharmakon*) was the poor themselves, who were scapegoated as *pharmakoi* in order to fight the plague. Here, the scheme is the inverse: cohesion and health are restored in the recognition that those exploited and excluded are loved in a preferential way by God and entitled to the medicine dispensed by Guadalupe. A final point about the nature of the medicinal spring at Tepeyac is that, like the healings of the Gospel, it is not reducible to worldly effect. That is, even if a devotee of Guadalupe dies—and all of us will—it does not signal defeat. Rather, in Christ is found that kind of life over which the plagues of this world have no control.

---

did not experience the ravages of the war in Yugoslavia.

49. Ita y Parra, 18.

Guadalupe and Remedios: Rivals or Collaborators?

The final theme of the sermon is the one that most clearly demonstrates the departure from the dynamics of scapegoating and sacrificial resolution. Ita y Parra has the obvious opportunity to create a kind of mass unity for Guadalupe over against Remedios. No doubt, this is complicated, and the defeat of Remedios would not bring a clear cohesion but also some intense division. But even if part of Ita y Parra's motivation is to construct a collaboration between the two such that Spaniards, *criollos* and Indians all feel included, then this too is a signal that a different kind of solidarity is being sought. And certainly in the face of the plague, solidarity is necessary for the restoration of health. People will need to work together, joined in common cause and commitment. Perhaps in the end it was this solidarity, forged in the fire of intense Guadalupan devotion, that caused the *matlazahuatl* to subside. We simply do not have the data to make a scientific conclusion. But in Ita y Parra's complex theory about how Remedios is working to save "in secrecy" while Guadalupe works "in public"[50] we might have a clue to help explain how public health efforts can be coextensive with divine intervention. That is, the sermon makes clear that in understanding God we cannot operate from an assumption of singular, direct causality. As he shows in quoting St. Paul that the visible world helps us "fathom" the invisible, Ita y Parra presents a sophisticated theory of causality in which the divine and the human do not compete.

The above theological formulations are intended to take seriously the message of Ita y Parra, delivered in 1737 in the midst of one of the greatest challenges Mexico has experienced in its history. And so it seems in order at least to note the current plague in that land: the drug war. With some sixty thousand lives lost between 2006 and 2012 alone, the conflict became more lethal than the wars in Iraq and Afghanistan during that time. Electoral and popular protest of the militarization of the conflict did arise, leading Mexican officials to propose new strategies. On numerous occasions, thousands have taken to the streets. And yet these processions were different than the pilgrimages of 1737; while images of Guadalupe are omnipresent in Mexico, the public gatherings were often not conducted under her banner. In fact, the Church has largely been absent from the conversations about the proper response to the scourge of drug trafficking. Part of the reason involves understandable fear, since many activists who have spoken out have

---

50. Ibid., 21.

been targeted and killed by cartels. A more unfortunate, and lesser, reason is the involvement of some clergy with "narcolimosnas," by which their struggling parishes receive assistance from wealthy drug lords. In either case, what is clear is that the voice of the Church could play an important role in the country's healing. And if any cues are taken from the sermon of Padre Bartolomé Felipe de Ita y Parra during the *matlazahuatl* of 1737, the church's voice could be prophetic. Following Ita y Parra, especially in the Girardian key I suggest, this would mean advancing a strategy that seeks the restoration of social unity and relief from the drug plague without this being achieved through the creation of new and more victims. In this way, at the center of this campaign would be Guadalupe, la Madre de Salud.

BIBLIOGRAPHY

Brading, D. A. *Mexican Phoenix: Our Lady of Guadalupe; Image and Tradition across Five Centuries.* Cambridge: Cambridge University Press, 2001.

———, ed. *Siete Sermones Guadalupanos (1709–1765).* Mexico City: Centro de Estudios de Historia de Mexico, Condumex, 1994.

Girard, René. *I See Satan Fall Like Lightning.* Maryknoll, NY: Orbis, 2001.

6

The Guadalupan Covenant
An Evaluation of the *Nican mopohua* in Light of the Ancient Jewish Tradition

Colleen Cross

IN THE OLD TESTAMENT, the notion of covenant extends beyond that of an agreement between God and God's people, or in the case of the Noahic covenant, God and all of creation. The covenant is revelatory in nature, a gift of God's self in history that more fully reveals who God is and God's plan for salvation. In the same manner, the apparition of our Lady of Guadalupe as told through the *Nican mopohua* is not just a concrete expression of God's love and saving power in history. In many ways, it is the self-revelation of Mary. Through this ultimate gift of self, we come to see Guadalupe for who she is; she is our mother, we are her children. Offering this unconditional, gratuitous gift of love, Guadalupe forms a covenant with all of creation. In her choice of the indigenous Juan Diego, she challenges not only the sins of the conqueror but the sins of the conquered. Through her motherhood, all are raised to a status of equality, where the *imago Dei* of each is fully illuminated as we are transformed in her love.

Contemporary theological scholarship has uncovered a variety of themes in the *Nican mopohua* speaking to topics of evangelization, conversion, and justification by grace, among others. One of the most important and well known is that of inculturated evangelization. In 2002, Pope John Paul II declared that the Guadalupe event, "'meant the beginning of evangelization with a vitality that surpassed all expectations. Christ's message, through his Mother, took up the central elements of the indigenous culture, purified

the guadalupan covenant

them and gave them the definitive sense of salvation.' Consequently Guadalupe and Juan Diego have a deep ecclesial and missionary meaning and are a model of perfectly inculturated evangelization."[1] Through her identification with the Indian Juan Diego, Guadalupe effectively challenges the slavery and victimization of the indigenous peoples wrought by the Spanish conquest.[2] In her apparition we see the message of the Gospel incarnated in indigenous narrative and imagery.[3] In this "perfectly inculturated evangelization," Guadalupe speaks to both the indigenous and the Spanish, calling both groups to a faithful and authentic conversion. "Her message not only converted the indigenous peoples from practices like human sacrifice but also demanded that Spanish Catholics repent of their ethnocentrism and violence."[4] In this manner, "what comes to be incarnated in relationship to the Guadalupan event is a new way of being for the church, a way that synthesizes both old and new, both European and Mexican-indigenous, into a new ecclesial reality altogether, a reality concretely expressed in the European-indigenous narrative and iconographic synthesis represented by Guadalupe herself."[5] Through Guadalupe we come not only to a new inculturated evangelization, but a new ecclesial reality.

In the formation of this new reality the question of conversion takes on a significant importance. The Guadalupe event emphasizes the essential nature of an affective discipleship foundational to an authentic conversion, requiring a re-orientation of one's whole being to the Gospel message. In the context of the Guadalupan apparitions, such a conversion requires all to love the Juan Diegos of this world, making a preferential option for those who have been victimized and oppressed by society, seeking a vision of justice grounded in right relationship. In speaking of this conversion, Timothy Matovina states, "Thus the *Nican Mopohua* encompasses the message that discipleship requires listening to the voice of the forgotten and

---

1. Pope John Paul II, "Canonization of Juan Diego Cuauhtlatoatzin." The pope was quoting a statement of the Mexican Episcopate in this homily in Mexico City on July 31, 2002.

2. Matovina, "Theologies of Guadalupe," 89–90. See also Elizondo, *Guadalupe*, 88–99; Siller Acuña, *Flor y canto*; Rodriguez, *Our Lady of Guadalupe*; Nebel, *Santa María Tonantzin*.

3. Matovina, "Theologies of Guadalupe," 89–90. See also Elizondo, *Guadalupe*, 25–78; Siller Acuña, *Flor y canto*; Rodriguez, *Our Lady of Guadalupe*; Nebel, *Santa María Tonantzin*.

4. Matovina, "Theologies of Guadalupe," 90.

5. Johnson, *Virgin of Guadalupe*.

marginalized, defending and helping them to sense their dignity as God's sons and daughters, and preferentially choosing them as the recipients of the church's proclamation of the gospel, service, and struggle for a more just social order."[6] At the same time however, this theme of conversion is not limited to a preferential option for the poor. Fundamentally, true conversion requires that we not only recognize the image of God in others but also in ourselves. Theologian Virgilio Elizondo articulates this concept, emphasizing that through Guadalupe

> All persons are called to conversion from that which imprisons them and robs them of the fullness of life; from that which enslaves them and keeps them from being free children of God; from that which blinds them and keeps them from appreciating themselves and others as God appreciates each one. Conversion is the great equalizer, for it calls everyone to the life and freedom of the children of God.[7]

The beauty of the Guadalupan event is that it not only called Bishop Juan de Zumárraga from a place of sinful pride, turning from religious ethnocentrism, but that it called Juan Diego out of self-abasement into the recognition of his dignity and worth as a child of God. In the gift of Guadalupe all are called to a place of authentic freedom where the fullness of the *imago Dei* is made known.

One argument asserts that Guadalupe, as this efficacious sign, can be interpreted as an expression of justification by grace through faith.[8] In the unconditional love and gift of grace that she brings, Guadalupe herself becomes a grace-filled gift, a concrete manifestation of God's overwhelming love for us. She is so special precisely because she is not necessary, and it is in this reality and the acceptance of this gift that Juan Diego is in turn able to freely respond. According to Maxwell Johnson, "that this gift is received 'through faith' is surely exemplified in the response of Juan Diego, who, like Abraham and countless prophets in the Hebrew Bible before him, interprets

---

6. Matovina, "Theologies of Guadalupe," 82.

7. Elizondo, *Guadalupe*, 87.

8. Citing the works of other contemporary theologians to undergird his claim, Maxwell Johnson states, "If the God revealed in the Guadalupan narrative is none other than 'the God-who-is-for-us' ([Orlando] Espín), characterized by 'a maternal presence, consoling, nurturing, offering unconditional love, comforting' and 'brimming over with gentleness, loving kindness, and forgiveness' as an 'unconditional and grace-filled gift to the people' (Jeanette Rodriguez), then it is precisely a proclamation of the God who justifies 'by grace alone.'" Johnson, *Virgin of Guadalupe*, 151.

the guadalupan covenant

this encounter as a call to his own prophetic ministry both to his own people and to the governing (ecclesiastical) authorities to whom he was sent."[9] And when through faith, we also accept this gift, our own encounters with Guadalupe in turn become a call to a more authentic conversion.

Although the *Nican mopohua* has been read in light of the aforementioned themes, it has not been read through the lens of covenant. Such an examination is critical for Guadalupan scholarship, particularly in light of the problematic notions of national covenant, divine retribution, and covenant renewal that arose vis-à-vis the national cult of Guadalupe in Mexico and among Mexican exiles in the United States in the nineteenth and early twentieth centuries. With the publication of the written accounts of the Guadalupe encounter, primarily the *Imagen de la Virgen María* written by Miguel Sánchez in 1648, the initial foundation for such sentiments was created. The realities of Eurocentrism and patriarchy that accompanied the Spanish conquest of the New World fed into the belief of a divine plan for this new Mexican nation as the New Israel and the center of Christian salvation. Many took the appearance of Our Lady of Guadalupe as a legitimation of such sentiments, believing that she came to extend her patronage to, and establish a covenant with, the Mexican people in a special way, "her chosen people, the beautiful Mexican nation."[10] This particular notion of chosenness can be problematic, as her patronage becomes co-opted for nationalist purposes, diminishing the claims that her love and care are universal.[11]

In the same manner, this problematic notion of national covenant then fosters sentiments of divine retribution and covenant renewal, denying the gratuitous and unconditional nature of Guadalupe's patronage and instead connecting it to an idea of quid pro quo exchange based on loyalty to Guadalupe, to God, and to the Mexican nation. For example, a connection between Our Lady of Guadalupe and Mexican nationalism is highlighted in the words of the influential nineteenth-century author Ignacio Manuel Altamirano. Writing of the importance of Guadalupe in Mexican life, Altamirano says, "the day that the cult of the Indian Virgin disappears, the Mexican

---

9. Ibid.

10. Clergy at the San Fernando Cathedral in San Antonio, Texas. Eve of the Feast of Our Lady of Guadalupe, December 11, 1931. In Matovina, *Guadalupe and Her Faithful*, 96–97.

11. Matovina, "Theologies of Guadalupe," 88.

nationality will also disappear."¹² When Mexico and its people experienced conflict and discord, such as the Mexican American War (1846–1848), the Mexican Revolution (1910–1917), and even in instances of internal religious conflict, this problematic notion of national covenant led Mexicans to believe that their suffering was the result of a fractured relationship with Guadalupe. Mexican leaders—religious and secular—and many Mexican devotees have contended in time of national difficulty that Guadalupe left them, denying them her patronage, or even that she was a direct participant in the violence against them.

Intertwined with this belief in divine retribution is that of covenant renewal—if the faithful turn back to Guadalupe, she will bless them again and her covenant with the Mexican nation and all of its people will be renewed. This idea was particularly salient among the Mexican exiles residing in the United States at the beginning of the twentieth century. In his sermon delivered on the Guadalupe feast in San Antonio in 1914, Archbishop Francisco Plancarte y Navarette of Linares urged "the people of Mexico to return to an adoration and supplication of Our Lady of Guadalupe as a means of obtaining peace in their country."¹³ Rather than a gratuitous gift for all peoples, Guadalupe's love and patronage become limited and conditional, intimately linked with the Mexican nation and only offered if she has been satisfied by their faithfulness.

Clearly, particular interpretations of this covenantal conception have proved highly problematic, fostering a nationalism that encompassed belief in a retributive model of divine favor. This, however, is not the notion of covenant that is present in the *Nican mopohua*. Evaluating the text in light of the ancient Jewish tradition, two examples emerge that assist in redefining the Guadalupan apparition: the Noahic and Mosaic covenants made in the Old Testament. While there are many other significant examples of covenant in the Old Testament, including the Abrahamic and the Davidic, this paper will focus on the initial covenant that YHWH makes in the Hebrew Scriptures with all of humanity, the Noahic, and the most prominent covenant of the Hebrew Scriptures, the Mosaic. Representing a conditional model through the bestowal of the divine law, the Mosaic covenant states, "I will be your God, and you will be my people" (Lev 26:12).¹⁴ In contrast,

---

12. Altamirano, paraphrased and reprinted in *La Prensa*, in Matovina, *Guadalupe and Her Faithful*, 116–17.

13. Matovina, *Guadalupe and Her Faithful*, 117.

14. New American Bible Revised Edition. All translations from NABRE unless

the guadalupan covenant

the Noahic covenant is an unconditional, gratuitous offer of love. These models present an interesting case for examination. One is limited, the other is universal; one is conditional, the other is an unconditional, gratuitous offer. When viewed in light of these covenant models, Our Lady of Guadalupe can be seen as a combination of the two. She embodies the relationality of the Mosaic covenant—I will be your Mother and you will be my children—and, analogous to the Noahic covenant, she presents her gift in an unconditional manner, a reality that has significant implications for her mission and message.

There are important elements in the *Nican mopohua* that allow for a creative reading of the text in light of the ideas of covenant in the ancient Jewish tradition, with obvious extensions into the Christian notion of covenant which Christians received from their Jewish roots. Extending beyond the notion of an agreement between two parties, the conception of covenant in the Old Testament was inherently revelatory in nature. Through God's actions, we come to a deeper understanding not only of salvation history but also of who God is. In the same manner, covenant speaks to us on this deeper level, unveiling who we are called to be before God.

The Noahic covenant is inherently one of creation and rebirth. Following the flood in Genesis, the process of renewal is forever changed as God promises to never again bring the waters of chaos upon creation.[15]

> See, I am now establishing my covenant with you and your descendants after you and with every living creature that was with you: all the birds, and the various tame and wild animals that were with you and came out of the ark. I will establish my covenant with you, that never again shall all bodily creatures be destroyed by the waters of a flood; there shall not be another flood to devastate the earth (Gen 9:9–11).

The Noahic covenant is unconditional. Rather than a standard covenant formula that presents a set of stipulations, structured in the form of conditional blessings and curses, the Noahic covenant requires nothing from those with whom it was made.

Further, God promises never to reject the covenant, regardless of how humanity acts. "When the LORD smelled the sweet odor, he said to himself: 'Never again will I doom the earth because of man, since the desires of

---

otherwise noted. For an in-depth examination of covenant in the Old Testament, please see Levenson, *Sinai and Zion*.

15. The text of the Noahic covenant can be found in Genesis 8:20—9:17.

man's heart are evil from the start; nor will I ever again strike down all living beings, as I have done. As long as the earth lasts, seedtime and harvest, cold and heat, summer and winter, and day and night shall not cease'" (Gen 8:21–22). A final essential element is that the covenant extends not only to the Hebrews, but to all peoples and all of creation.[16]

The Mosaic covenant, in contrast, closely relates to the covenant formulary of the ancient Hittite Suzerain treaties.[17] This formal agreement between unequals is a conditional system of blessings and curses, requiring that the Israelites obey God's commands in order for the covenant to be valid.[18] The following biblical citation from the Mosaic covenant typifies this type of treaty, "Now, if you obey me completely and keep my covenant, you will be my treasured possession among all peoples, though all the earth is mine. You will be to me a kingdom of priests, a holy nation" (Exod 19:5–6). Disobedience, however, results not only in the removal of divine favor, but often takes the form of a curse. "But if you do not heed me and do not keep all these commandments, if you reject my precepts and spurn my decrees, refusing to obey all my commandments and breaking my covenant, then I, in turn, will give you your deserts. I will punish you with terrible woes—with wasting and fever to dim the eyes and sap the life" (Lev 26:14–16).[19] It can be seen that the covenant is one of relationality. Following the promise made to Moses, God fulfills the statement, "I will take you as my own people, and you shall have me as your God" (Exod 6:7) and "I will set my Dwelling among you, and will not disdain you. Ever present in your midst, I will be your God and you will be my people," (Lev 26:11–12) formally calling the Hebrews to become God's chosen people.[20]

In this manner, the notion of covenant in the Old Testament extends beyond a revelation of God's self, but fundamentally reveals who we as believers, as people, are called to be before God. Forged at Sinai, the Mosaic covenant calls forth a profound understanding of relationality. Established on this comprehension of the inequality between God and the Hebrews,

---

16. Genesis 9:10.

17. For more information refer to Levenson, *Sinai and Zion*, 26.

18. The stipulations of this covenant are generally seen in terms of the Ten Commandments (Exod 20:3–17). For more detailed list of blessings and curses, please see also Lev 26.

19. The curses for breaking the covenant are listed in Lev 26:14–39.

20. It is important to note that while this covenant is conditional, God remains faithful and does not make the covenant void. God has chosen Israel as His own, a promise that is fulfilled despite Israel's disobedience.

discipleship[21] becomes a condition of the covenant, calling them to recognize their utter dependence on God. The fulfillment of every person, and society as a whole, is intrinsically linked with the divine law. Each person not only has the right, but also the duty of participation in striving toward adherence of the Law and the fullness of being God's people. In contrast, the Noahic covenant can be seen as a gratuitous gift of love. God's promise, manifest in the rainbow,[22] reveals that all of creation is beloved by God. Discipleship is not a condition, but a freely given gift, whereby we respond to God's love with our own.

Examining the *Nican mopohua* vis-à-vis this lens of covenant calls us to examine what is revealed through Guadalupe's encounter with Juan Diego: what we learn about God, Guadalupe, and ourselves in her apparition. The text of the *Nican mopohua* begins with Juan Diego seeking "the things of God and God's messages" (6).[23] One powerful element in this narrative is that he was answered in a way he had neither planned for, nor expected. In the Guadalupe experience Juan Diego is drawn into the tremendous, overflowing love of Guadalupe, and by extension God. And through this encounter, Juan Diego is transformed in both mind and heart. The Guadalupan apparition, understood as a gratuitous offer of self by the Virgin Mary, is then fundamentally one of transformation. And it is within Juan Diego's experience that this covenant which Guadalupe offers becomes more fully revealed—within the mystical experience of Guadalupe through the transformation of the created world, her offer of motherhood to all, and the creative reconstruction of identity for both conquered and conqueror. Like Juan Diego, we, as readers and believers, are drawn into the covenant, discovering the tremendous, passionate love of Guadalupe and are ourselves transformed through this mystical encounter with the loving, ever-Virgin Mother of God.

Juan Diego's encounter with Guadalupe begins with music, the "beautiful and alluring singing of the birds."[24] The text reads, "He heard singing on the summit of the hill: as if different precious birds were singing and their songs would alternate, as if the hill was answering them" (6). In Nahuatl

---

21. Understood not only as right belief, but also right action.

22. Gen 9:12–17.

23. "The Text of the *Nican Mopohua*," translated by Elizondo in *Guadalupe*. The quotation above as well as further quotations from the *Nican mopohua* are cited in context with page numbers from this source.

24. Elizondo, *Guadalupe*, 35.

thought, music provided a manner for contemplation and communication with the divine, while birds represented a mediation between heaven and earth.[25] In this way, we see that Juan Diego is drawn into the encounter with Guadalupe even before she reveals herself. Through the beautiful singing of the birds, he comes to recognize that he is in the presence of someone/something heavenly and a divine message is to be communicated. Responding to this realization with wonder and humility, Juan Diego says "By chance do I deserve this? Am I worthy of what I am hearing? Maybe I am dreaming? Maybe I only see this in my dreams?" (6). In this manner, the author establishes Juan Diego's perceived inferiority. Although Our Lady of Guadalupe has chosen one deemed insignificant by society to be her messenger, his internalization of such sentiments is intimated in his response.

In this introduction to the Guadalupan covenant we are presented an interesting contrast to the covenant formulary of Sinai. The Mosaic covenant begins with a preamble where God identifies himself. "I am the LORD your God, who brought you out of the land of Egypt, out of the house of slavery" (Exod 20:2). By highlighting this relationship with Israel where God has rescued them by frustrating their enemies time and again, the inequality between these two parties is emphasized. Conversely, in the Guadalupan covenant it is Juan Diego who wishes to establish his inequality. Guadalupe, however, seeks him out precisely to greet him in his full humanity. Her initial presence is made known not through a profound declaration of her meritorious actions, but rather in a gift of beauty, the singing of the birds. And in this manner she foreshadows a prominent theme of the covenant she seeks to establish—a conversion of heart where all, including the victimized and subjugated, will recognize their equality in the *imago Dei*.

As the singing of the birds comes to an end, he hears his name being called out, "Dignified Juan, dignified Juan Diego" (7). Rather than highlighting his lowliness, Guadalupe's first words to Juan Diego serve to elevate him, bringing him deeper into relationship with her and opening his heart to the message she is imparting. As a result, his heart is quieted and he is able to follow the call, desiring to know she who is calling him close.[26] Here Guadalupe announces her presence through the transformation of nature rather than a direct verbal address.

---

25. Ibid., 6.

26. See *Nican mopohua*, #14. "Then he dared to go where he is being called. His heart was in no way disturbed, and in no way did he experience any fear; on the contrary, he felt very good, very happy."

> And the rock and the cliffs where she was standing, upon receiving the rays like arrows of light, appeared like precious emeralds, appeared like jewels; the earth glowed with the splendors of the rainbow. The mesquites, the cacti, and the weeds that were all around appeared like feathers of the quetzal, and the stems looked like turquoise; the branches, the foliage, and even the thorns sparkled like gold (7).

Instead of choosing a physical manifestation evoking power and might, Guadalupe makes her presence known through beauty. Like the rainbow, the beautiful music and flowers representative of the Guadalupan event signify not only this gratuitous offering of love, but also the rebirth and renewal of all of creation. And it is this rebirth and renewal that is central to the covenant she establishes. In the transformation of the physical world, she echoes God's love of creation seen in the Noahic covenant and initiates the transformation of Juan Diego, challenging not only his historical marginalization under the oppressive paradigms of the conquerors, but also the "debilitating self-abasement"[27] he has internalized. In his reaction, he begins to respond to this efficacious sign of love, returning it in kind not only to Guadalupe but also to himself.[28] "He bowed before her, heard her thought and word, which were exceedingly re-creative, very ennobling, alluring, producing love" (7). And in this manner, she begins to illuminate the *imago Dei* that has been dimmed, and even defiled, in Juan Diego.[29]

This gratuitous self-offering of Guadalupe continues as she identifies herself to Juan Diego as Mary, the Ever-Virgin Mother of God, making her request known. In the narrative, Guadalupe states,

> I very much want and ardently desire that my hermitage be erected in this place. In it I will show and give to all people all my love, my compassion, my help, and my protection, because I am your merciful mother and the mother of all the nations that live on this earth who would love me, who would speak with me, who would search for me, and who would place their confidence in me. There I will hear their laments and remedy and cure all their miseries, misfortunes, and sorrows (8).

---

27. Matovina, "Theologies of Guadalupe," 83.

28. It must be noted that Juan Diego's internal transformation does not reach a stage of completion until the end of the narrative.

29. Reference to the Latin American Episcopal Conference (CELAM) at Puebla. Translated in *On Job*, Gutierrez, xiii.

She grounds her request in the desire to become the mother of all nations, making all peoples her children. This connection with Guadalupe as mother is essential as it not only establishes a relationality between Guadalupe and Juan Diego, like that established at Sinai, but emphasizes that this covenant with Juan Diego, and all the children on the New World whom she adopts as her own, is one of abounding love. Like all mothers, her identity is intrinsically related with that of her children.[30] She does not make a preferential option for the Spanish conquerors, the Mexican nation, or even the indigenous. Rather, she makes an option for all peoples, becoming the mother of all.

This is further evidenced by the identification she provides to Juan Diego when they first meet. "Know and be certain in your heart, my most abandoned son, that I am the Ever-Virgin Holy Mary, Mother of the God of Great Truth, Téotl, of the One through Whom We Live, the Creator of Persons, the owner of What is Near and Together, of the Lord of Heaven and Earth" (7–8). According to Elizondo, her use of these names is an important revelation in itself. Although these titles for the divine were present in preconquest Nahuatl theology, Spanish evangelizers rejected them. Her use of these holy names for God challenges this rejection and re-establishes their authenticity and veracity in worship.[31] Theologically this identification of Guadalupe with Nahuatl theology has significant implications. Spanish belief in their call to establish and evangelize this new land, believing that they were bringing the light of the Gospel to a world steeped in sin, rationalized and legitimated their conquest. However, this identification of Guadalupe with Nahuatl theology questions the view that the New World had been denied all Gospel truths until the Spanish conquest.[32] It also rejects the problematic notions of national covenant that arise in relation to the national cult of Guadalupe. By inviting all peoples into this relationship, Guadalupe not only universalizes her covenant but calls us all into relationship with God and with one another.

In the traditional covenant formulary, following a statement of the past relationship of the parties "I am the LORD your God, who brought

---

30. See Goizueta, *Caminemos Con Jesús*. In this work, Goizueta articulates a theology of accompaniment whereby we recognize that relationship is a constitutive element of who we are and respond to this relationality by making a preferential option for the poor.

31. Elizondo, *Guadalupe*, 8.

32. In speaking to the presence of Gospel truths I am referring to the "seeds of truth" found in other religions, emphasized in the documents of Vatican II.

the guadalupan covenant

you out of the land of Egypt, out of the house of slavery" (Exod 20:2), the ruler would formally stipulate the terms of the agreement. In the Mosaic covenant God promises the Israelites, "I will take you as my own people, and I will be your God" (Exod 6:7). This covenant of relationality and the blessings that arise through it are, however, conditional, requiring explicit action on the part of the Israelites for the covenant to be fulfilled. If the Guadalupan apparition, read through the lens of the *Nican mopohua*, is to be understood in light of the Sinai covenant, one might expect her self-identification and declaration of intent to be followed by a formal agreement. However, like the Noahic covenant, such stipulations are absent in the Guadalupan encounter. Guadalupe's gift of love requires no response; her love will transform us if only we allow it to. This is precisely what makes it so profound—discipleship is not a condition, but a freely given gift in response to her love. And although Juan Diego's response is not required, the covenant is not one-sided. To be realized in its fullness it requires a dynamic interplay between Guadalupe and Juan Diego, between Guadalupe and all of us. In order to be fully transformed, we must accept her love and let it bring us into deeper conversion.

Through Juan Diego's second and third encounters with the Virgin we see how difficult this transformation truly is. By accepting Guadalupe's love and motherhood, Juan Diego is called to a creative reinterpretation of self. However, having internalized the marginalization experienced at the hands of the conquerors, Juan Diego implicitly participates in the diminishment of the *imago Dei*. Matovina writes, "In the *Nican Mopohua* his greatest sin is a lack of self-worth, an internalization of the effects of the conquest, particularly the conquerors' presumption that the natives were inferior or even subhuman. Ultimately Juan Diego's internalization of the conquerors' judgments and stereotypes led him to not accept that he too was made in God's image and likeness."[33] Having just been rejected by Bishop Zumárraga, Juan Diego questions his worth and efficacy as the messenger of Guadalupe. He believes that her message had not been accomplished, her temple not built, because of his social status. "You, my most abandoned Daughter, my Child, my Lady, and my Queen, send me to a place where I do not belong. Forgive me, I will cause pain to your countenance and to your heart; I will displease you and fall under your wrath, my Lady and my Owner" (10). Like Moses at the burning bush,[34] one of Juan Diego's greatest obstacles in bearing Gua-

33. Matovina, "Theologies of Guadalupe," 82.
34. Exod 3:11; 4:1.

119

dalupe's messages is not the bishop, but himself and a lack of confidence in his chosenness.

Although this sin of self-abasement is apparent in Juan Diego's interaction with the Virgin, she does not chastise him. Rather, she disputes these feelings of inadequacy, emphasizing that it is precisely through his mediation that her desire will be realized. "Listen, my most abandoned son, know well in your heart that there are not a few of my servants and messengers to whom I could give the mandate of taking my thought and my word so that my will may be accomplished. But it is absolutely necessary that you personally go and speak about this, and that precisely through your mediation and help, my wish and my desire be realized" (10). According to Elizondo, the temple that Guadalupe wishes to have built speaks as much to an eschatological vision of hope as it does to a physical shrine.[35] The reign of God will erupt into this world not through the rich and the powerful, but rather through those who have been rejected, marginalized, and 'othered' by society.[36] Guadalupe is a concrete expression of God's love, and her own, made manifest for us. In the concrete, she prefigures this larger covenant that transcends time and place to be realized in the hearts of all believers. Rather than dismiss Juan Diego, she uses him as a vehicle to make her message—her love—known. And it is only through her love that Juan Diego is able to fully respond to this call of affective discipleship. "In my name *you* will make him [Bishop Zumárraga] know, make him listen well to my wish and desire" (11). In electing Juan Diego to be her messenger and orchestrating an encounter with the bishop, she begins to bring Juan Diego not only into right relationship with the bishop, but with himself. In this covenant, in this ultimate gift of self, Guadalupe draws us all into this affective and transforming love, calling us to right relationship with God, with others, and with ourselves.

However, this journey of transformation is a process for both Juan Diego and Bishop Zumárraga. Before they are brought to this place of equality in right relationship, both Juan Diego and Juan de Zumárraga must challenge the convictions they hold of themselves and of each other. For Juan Diego, this requires going to the bishop a second time. Although he promises the Virgin that he will bring her message to the bishop again, he still doubts his chosenness, "I will go to do your will. But it could well be that I will not be listened to; and if I am listened to, possibly I will not be

---

35. Elizondo, *Guadalupe*, 10–11 n. 17.
36. Ibid.

the guadalupan covenant

believed" (11). After a second lengthy interview with the bishop, he is again denied, told that his word and message are not sufficient. In order for the bishop's heart to be moved, he requests a sign from the Virgin.

Guadalupe provides such a sign in beautiful Castilian flowers, often depicted as roses, that he discovers on the summit of Tepeyac.[37] The flowers were much more than the symbol that allowed her message to be heard and her mission to be accomplished. It is in this sign that Juan Diego first comes into a place of confident acceptance in his role as chosen messenger. In the same manner, this gift of flowers calls the bishop into authentic conversation with Juan Diego, seeing Juan Diego for the first time not as a lowly Indian, but rather as the messenger of the Blessed Ever-Virgin Mary. In this moment where Juan Diego is seen not for his social status but for the true dignity and worth associated with his chosenness, the transformation central to the Guadalupan covenant—seeing ourselves and others in the fullness of the *imago Dei*—is prefigured.

Yet this fullness of this transformation is not accomplished until Guadalupe allows herself to become a living sign, sacramentally present on Juan Diego's *tilma* (cloak). In the words of the *Nican mopohua*, "In that very moment she painted herself: the precious image of the Ever-Virgin Holy Mary, Mother of the God Téotl, appeared suddenly, just as she is today and is kept in her precious home, in her hermitage of Tepeyac, which is called Guadalupe" (20). In this ultimate gift of self, Juan Diego and the bishop are together drawn into a mystical encounter of Guadalupe, transformed through her love to a place of equality and dignity. It is in this encounter with Guadalupe's image that we experience the same transformation, called from our sin to a place of right relationship, with God, with Guadalupe, and with each other. Ultimately, what Guadalupe reveals is a covenant of gratuitous, unconditional love with each of us and with all of the cosmos—a covenant that is reaffirmed every time we see her picture and experience her presence.

At its heart, the Guadalupan covenant is one of relationality. In her encounter with Juan Diego, Guadalupe seeks to enter into relationship, offering her love and patronage. Similar to the Mosaic covenant establishing a bond between God and the Israelite people, Guadalupe wishes to become one with the principal protagonists of the *Nican mopohua*, Juan Diego and Juan de Zumárraga. However, her desire to be in relation does not end

---

37. *Nican mopohua*, #81–87.

there; through the gift of her image, she invites all who gaze on her into relationship as well.

Foundational to the Guadalupan covenant is the gratuitous self-offering made not only to Juan Diego, but to all of creation. While historically Guadalupe has been claimed by all sides—from the Spanish who wanted to use her to control the Indians, to the Indians who saw her as a symbol of, and call to, liberation—Guadalupe cannot be seen to particularize some, but rather must be recognized as the universal mother of all. Although Juan Diego is indigenous, and a member of this new Mexican nation, Guadalupe does not make her covenant just with the Mexican nation or solely with Christian believers. She makes it with all of her children. In this manner, the universal and unconditional nature of the Noahic covenant is echoed. She truly becomes the mother of all.

This overflowing love central to the Guadalupan covenant is evidenced through the theme of healing present in the Guadalupan event. In Juan Diego's third encounter with the Virgin, he relates to Guadalupe that a great illness has befallen his uncle Juan Bernardino and he fears for his uncle's life. Speaking to his concern, Guadalupe assures him:

> Listen and hear well in your heart, my most abandoned son: that which scares you and troubles you is nothing; do not let your countenance and heart be troubled; do not fear that sickness or any other sickness or anxiety. Am I not here, your mother? Are you not under my shadow and my protection? Am I not your source of life? Are you not in the hollow of my mantle where I cross my arms? Who else do you need? Let nothing trouble you or cause you sorrow (15–16).

The words of Guadalupe speak to us on a deeper level. Just as Juan Diego's uncle, Juan Bernardino, is physically healed in this offering of love, she offers her healing to each and every one of us. For some, it is physical healing. However, the greatest gift of healing that she provides is a creative reconstruction of identity. Like Juan Diego and Bishop Zumárraga, we are called out of our sinfulness into the fullness of the *imago Dei*. We must not only see the crucified and risen face of Christ in the other, but in ourselves.

> It is the experience of this unconditional and unmerited grace of God that not only rehabilitates but even re-creates all people so as to bring them into a new common household, into the new family bonds beyond all the blood bonds of this world. . . . Through her, one experiences a new space of love in which everyone is welcomes,

everyone is respected, everyone is valued, and everyone is listened to. But even more, one experiences in one's heart a new freedom and joy of living, a new serenity and peace, a new reason for living that heals and liberates from the sufferings of this world.[38]

Through this unconditional, gratuitous offering of self, Guadalupe makes the transformative love and grace of God known to all persons, allowing us to be re-created and brought into the fullness of the *imago Dei*.

Intimately connected with this theme of healing is the transformation of the physical world and the gratuitous gift of self she provides. Initially, Guadalupe uses this transformation of the natural world to announce her presence and draw Juan Diego into an authentic encounter with her. And when Juan Diego doubts his ability to carry out her message, she provides a sign in the form of roses for him to bring to the bishop. Such a transformation is a concrete expression of this love that she wishes to give to all of creation. Similar to the Noahic covenant, the Guadalupan covenant is not limited to human beings, it is a covenant with the whole earth. As God promised to sustain creation, refusing to let flood waters envelop and destroy the earth, Guadalupe seeks to bring all of creation into harmony with *imago Dei*. Through her love, not only is the physical world transformed, but in this transformation Juan Diego is drawn into a mystical experience of Guadalupe that, in many ways, can be seen as a prefigurement of the beatific vision—allowing Juan Diego to see himself as he is seen by God.

Examining the *Nican mopohua* in light of both the Mosaic and Noahic covenants allows for a creative integration that advances biblical notions of covenant and draws us into the Guadalupe narrative. Through her gratuitous gift of love, Guadalupe makes a covenant with both the conquered and the conqueror, offering herself to all. Juan Diego is the prototype of our response to Guadaupe—his discipleship is not required or forced; rather it is a gratuitous response to the love she offers. And while Guadalupe revealed herself to Juan Diego at Tepeyac, establishing this covenant, we are all invited to encounter her for she renews her covenant with each of us every time we see her image.

---

38. Elizondo, in Johnson, *Virgin of Guadalupe*, viii.

BIBLIOGRAPHY

Altamirano, Ignacio Manuel. "La Fiesta de Guadalupe." In *Testimonicos Históricos Guadalupanos*, edited by Ernesto de la Torre Villar and Ramiro Navarro de Anda, 1128–1210 and 1209–1210. Mexico City: Fondo de Cultura Económica, 1982.

Berlin, Adele, and Marc Zvi Brettler, eds. *The Jewish Study Bible*. Jewish Publication Society. Oxford: Oxford University Press, 2004.

Brading, D. A. *Mexican Phoenix: Our Lady of Guadalupe; Image and Tradition across Five Centuries*. Cambridge: Cambridge University Press, 2001.

Carillo y Ancona, Crescencio. "Sermon for Guadalupe coronation ceremony," October 12, 1895. In *Album de la coronación de la Sma. Virgen de Guadalupe*, edited by Victoriano Agüeros, appendix, vol. 2, 10–18. Mexico: El Tiempo, 1895–1896.

Elizondo, Virgilio. *Guadalupe: Mother of the New Creation*. Maryknoll, NY: Orbis, 1997.

Goizueta, Roberto. *Caminemos con Jesús: Toward a Hispanic/Latino Theology of Accompaniment*. Maryknoll, New York: Orbis, 1995.

Gutierrez, Gustavo. *On Job: God-Talk and the Suffering of the Innocent*. Maryknoll, NY: Orbis, 1987.

John Paul II, Pope. "Canonization of Juan Diego Cuauhtlatoatzin." Homily, Mexico City, July 31, 2002. www.vatican.va/holy_father/john_paul_ii/homilies/2002/documents/hf_jp-ii_hom_20020731_canonization-mexico_en.html

Johnson, Maxwell. *The Virgin of Guadalupe: Theological Reflections of an Anglo-Lutheran Liturgist*. Lanham, MD: Rowman and Littlefield, 2002.

Matovina, Timothy. *Guadalupe and Her Faithful: Latino Catholics in San Antonio, from Colonial Origins to the Present*. Baltimore: Johns Hopkins University Press, 2005.

———. "Theologies of Guadalupe: From the Spanish Colonial Era to Pope John Paul II." *Theological Studies* 70 (2009) 61–91.

7

Apocalypse at Tepeyac

Michael Anthony Abril

SOMETHING EXTRAORDINARY HAPPENED ON a hill on the outskirts of Mexico City in 1531. As explained by Virgilio Elizondo, time witnessed a unique historic event of divine revelation, which within the darkness of violent bloodshed and conquest announced the dawning of a new cosmic era, the birth of a new creation, a new humanity. On this hill, called Tepeyac, the Virgin Mary appeared to the lowly, servile Juan Diego in order to restore the dignity of his people and to reveal the prophetic call to the downtrodden to become instruments of the Gospel. In order to reveal God's love for the marginalized in a unique and monumental way, the Virgin of Guadalupe sent Juan Diego to the bishop and provided him with a miraculous image that appeared on Juan Diego's outer garment: the icon of Our Lady of Guadalupe. In view of the biblical origins of this image, "The Mexican event was not just another miracle, another apparition; it was the fulfillment of the prophecy of John the Apostle in the *Apocalypse*."[1]

In this way, Our Lady of Guadalupe is an *apocalyptic* icon, although Elizondo never explicitly refers to it as such. J. Matthew Ashley, in his excellent overview of theological apocalypticism, argues, "what is distinctive of apocalypticism is its willingness to assert a high degree of transparency of historical events to the saving will of God."[2] In this very sense, Elizondo's theology

---

1. Elizondo, *La Morenita*, 106. A good summary of Elizondo's theology of Guadalupe can be found in J. Rodriguez, "The Common Womb of the Americas: Virgilio Elizondo's Theological Reflection on Our Lady of Guadalupe." See also Rubén Rosario Rodríguez's interpretation from a Protestant perspective: "Beyond Word and Sacrament: A Reformed Protestant Engagement of Guadalupan Devotion." A collection of excerpts from Elizondo's works on Guadalupe can be found in *Virgilio Elizondo: Spiritual Writings*, 112–42.

2. Ashley, "Apocalypticism," 37.

of Guadalupe has a distinctively cosmic character, highlighting a universal revelation within a particular, limited historical event.³ The transcendent and ever-present love of God is revealed in a particular time and a place, and proclaims a mission for the downtrodden. If we understand "apocalypse" in its original and proper meaning as "revelation," then for Elizondo, Guadalupe is the unique Marian *apocalypse* of the new humanity.⁴

Apocalyptic not only reveals the transcendent significance of particular events within history, but also grounds the fundamental meaning of history itself. The event of divine in-breaking is the definitive manifestation of history's inner meaning, its relatedness to the God of love. The Guadalupe event, precisely as an event within and of history, at the same time reveals the cosmic unity of all history as definitively oriented toward its eschatological culmination in Christ. "This is not just a moment of history . . . We are now in a moment of cosmic time!"⁵ In view of Guadalupe, then, history attains its real character of facticity. It becomes more than a mere collection of isolated incidents. History, as the history of salvation, becomes a unified and organic narrative of Jesus's saving love made manifest in the compassion of his Mother.⁶

In light of Elizondo's theology, the event of Our Lady of Guadalupe must be reexamined in view of its apocalyptic implications. These reflections can be expanded by considering Miguel Sánchez's interpretation of the apparition and image in terms of Revelation 12. This analysis will open up important connections to contemporary apocalyptic thought, especially that of René Girard and Johann Baptist Metz. Against the commonplace assumption that apocalyptic cripples the this-worldly work of justice, Our

---

3. "Universal" here is best understood in Metz's sense of truth as that which is relevant for all subjects. Metz, *Faith in History and Society*, 69.

4. *Apocalypse* comes from the Greek ἀποκαλύπτειν, to uncover, reveal. The term's not altogether incorrect denotation of the end of the world derives from the title of the last book in the Bible, the Apocalypse of John, now typically called the book of Revelation. This book's meaning cannot be constricted to pertaining to the end of the world, nor thought of in terms of predictions of strictly categorical events of future history. Nevertheless, a theology of the apocalypse is best understood not merely in terms of a fundamental theology of revelation, but as a holistic theology that encapsulates both the *form* of revelation and its intrinsic relationship to the material *content* of the book of Revelation. Accordingly, although "apocalypse" is first and foremost "revelation" and not the end of the world or the associated violent cataclysm, an overly strict distinction between these categories would be misleading.

5. Elizondo, *Guadalupe*, 32; cf. Elizondo, "Bicultural Approach," 258.

6. Cf. Doak, *Reclaiming Narrative*, 193.

apocalypse at tepeyac

Lady of Guadalupe emphasizes the liberative aspect of apocalyptic, as God's Word mediated through the poor.

This discussion follows three major headings. The first briefly summarizes key elements of Elizondo's theology of Guadalupe, which provide an inlet toward an apocalyptic analysis of Guadalupe. Elizondo's arguments here implicitly frame precisely what is meant by the complex term "apocalyptic," a term which, because of its rich and controversial history, can only really be understood in view of its operation within a *specific*, particular theological retrieval. The second part begins by briefly presenting historical background on Miguel Sánchez's text, then highlights and expands upon apocalyptic themes from the major apparition accounts, following inspiration from Sánchez. The final part draws important links between Guadalupe, Girard, and Metz that illuminate the liberative meaning of the apocalypse.

ELIZONDO'S APOCALYPSE OF FLOWER AND SONG

Inspired by Pierre Teilhard de Chardin, Elizondo understands the Guadalupe event as a unique "breakthrough" in world history. "As in any breakthrough, it will not come about without much pain, suffering, turmoil, and confusion, for the introduction of something truly new is not easily understood or appreciated."[7] It is a *painful* moment of revelation, signifying the "birth pangs" of a new humanity emerging from the "womb" of Tepeyac.[8] The tension of this situation forms the background of Elizondo's theology of Guadalupe as divine revelation to the Americas, wherein "Divinity is erupting and speaking to them in a way they can understand."[9]

---

7. Elizondo, *Future Is Mestizo*, 101. Teilhard de Chardin's influence is reflected in Elizondo's theme of the "New Creation." García-Rivera, "Crossing Theological Borders," 249, 251; see also Elizondo, *Spiritual Writings*, 19.

8. Elizondo, *Guadalupe*, 38; Elizondo, *Future Is Mestizo*, 64. Cf. Rev 12:2. "Womb" apparently is drawn from Teilhard de Chardin, *Hymn of the Universe*, 16–17. Elizondo further uses this concept to relate the experience of the Guadalupan encounter with Mary's visitation of Elizabeth: Elizondo, "Converted by Beauty," 78.

9. Elizondo, "Mary and Evangelization in the Americas," 155.

New Frontiers in Guadalupan Studies

The Humanizing Form of Revelation

Contemporary theological analyses of Guadalupe make ample use of the early indigenous Nahuatl account of the apparition, the *Nican mopohua*, published in 1649 by Luis Laso de la Vega. The *Nican mopohua* expresses the revelatory character of the Guadalupe event in a unique way.[10] It speaks with an indigenous Nahua voice out of the situation of violence and conquest.[11] It accomplishes this precisely by opting for a manner of speech which, like the Bible, intrinsically opens itself up toward interpretation by mediating a superabundance of meaning through the aesthetic language of *flor y canto*, flower and song.[12] For the Nahuas, flower and song signified the aesthetics of sacred space, the language of the encounter with the divine.[13] To the degree to which the *form* of revelation belongs to the character of revelation itself, this communication articulates a theological aesthetics.[14] Elizondo explains:

---

10. For the *Nican mopohua*, see Elizondo, *Guadalupe*, 5–22. Elizondo's source is the theologically charged Spanish of Clodomiro Siller Acuña, *Flor y Canto del Tepeyac*. The Elizondo/Siller Acuña translation is helpfully literalistic, but not especially rigorous in terms of historical scholarship. A more scholarly translation from the Nahuatl can be found in Sousa et al., *Story of Guadalupe*. Its more fluid rendering takes account of the sense of Nahuatl idioms. One could thus argue that it is more 'faithful' to the meaning of the text. Nevertheless, this translation hides the formal character of the Nahuatl idiom, and risks overlooking its theological significance. Accordingly, Elizondo's text is utilized here.

11. Despite U.S. Latino theology's emphasis on popular religion as a *locus theologicus*, its theologians typically rely upon the objectivity of the historical text for many of their claims. See, for example, Espín, *Faith of the People*, 73–78. This (anachronistic) textual dependence is interesting, considering the fact that although broad traces of the account are common knowledge among Guadalupe devotees the explicit text of the *Nican mopohua* is not widely read. This appeal to the text is important, however, because it provides a *history* to the popular devotion, which not only grounds its lasting significance as more than a transitory event, but also forms connections to the broader bases of Latino spirituality: the history of Christian tradition mediated through Iberian culture as well as pre-Hispanic indigenous culture, religion, and idiom.

12. Cf. Collins, *Apocalyptic Imagination*, 282; Elizondo, "Mary and Evangelization," 155.

13. Elizondo, *Future Is Mestizo*, 63.

14. A number of recent works have attempted to articulate a U.S. Latino theological aesthetics, with greater or lesser success. Such attempts do not always clearly distinguish themselves from what Balthasar would term "aesthetic theology," rather than theological aesthetics, properly speaking. The best work in this area has been by Roberto Goizueta. See *Christ Our Companion*.

Guadalupe is not an isolated, abstract, doctrinal truth; neither is it a legal or moralistic truth. According to the Guadalupan vision, truth exists in the relational, the interconnected, the beautiful, and the melodic; it cannot be reduced to a single, essential element, for it is only in its totality, in its wholeness, that this truth can be perceived and appreciated. Ultimate truth cannot be corralled by definition; it can only be approximated through *flor y canto*.[15]

Guadalupe does not merely reveal an isolated, propositional statement about God, knowable in terms of objective correspondence. The organic, aesthetic character of Guadalupe reveals the character of revelation itself, as fundamentally oriented toward *cosmic* significance while demanding subjective, existential appropriation. "Guadalupe is the truth about truth itself."[16]

By opting to evangelize through *flor y canto*, Our Lady of Guadalupe eschews the violent model of the Spanish conquest, which was rooted in a reductively objective concept of truth.[17] Conquerors and conquered alike allowed the success of warfare to dictate the truthfulness of religion. Yet the truth of Guadalupe is incompatible with the language of violence. Her humble language of *flor y canto* repudiates the blending of violence with truth.[18]

Only in this way can divine revelation show itself in its proper character as a revelation of *love*. Mary's address to Juan Diego recognizes his dignity as a human person, which had been destroyed in the spirit of conquest.[19] Juan Diego undergoes a conversion, not from personal sin, but from the structural effects of sin which had led him to see himself as worthless. Mary invites Juan Diego to see himself with God's loving eyes.[20] Revelation is *humanizing*. It overcomes corrupt societal expectations about what it means to be human, which set Iberian existence as the standard of human dignity.[21] Guadalupe establishes the anthropological identity of the human being in relation to his or her prior and more radical relationship to the God of love.[22]

The revelation of love extends beyond the mere propositional *fact* of love. Guadalupe reveals love by making present the very *person* of the Virgin

15. Elizondo, *Guadalupe*, 116; see also León-Portilla, *Aztec Thought*, 182.
16. Elizondo, *Guadalupe*, 116.
17. Ibid., 76; see Doak, *Reclaiming Narrative*, 196–97.
18. Cf. León-Portilla, *Aztec Image of Self and Society*, 99.
19. Elizondo, *Guadalupe*, 51–53; see also Goizueta, "Resurrection at Tepeyac," 343.
20. Elizondo, *Guadalupe*, 90.
21. See ibid., 40.
22. Cf. Metz, *Faith in History*, 70.

Mary.[23] She is unlike the indigenous gods, who were beyond human knowledge and human relationships.[24] The content of Guadalupan devotion is more than a noetic teaching, a moral imperative, or an ethnic history. It is a relationship with the Mother of God, who through her appearance to Juan Diego, reveals herself as mother of all of the world's people.[25] Juan Diego's humanizing encounter is shared by people today all over the world, who encounter Mary through the beauty of the image of Guadalupe. Elizondo explains, "She is a sacred icon whose power is far beyond our abilities of comprehension but whose life-giving power and liberating influence are at the very core of our untiring struggles for survival and new life."[26]

A Precipitate Event

Fundamental to Elizondo's theology of revelation is the event-character of the divine self-communication. Just as the Incarnation proclaims the truth of the Gospel through the peculiarities of a historical Galilean living on the fringes of Jewish society, Guadalupe manifests God's love through a unique, dramatic event in the life of a poor indigenous Mexican, Juan Diego. Even the apparently incidental contingencies of this story invite interpretation.

Elizondo thus meditates on the temporal setting of the first apparition, which takes place "when it was still night," although "it was already beginning to dawn."[27] Elizondo explains, "The joy of Easter, the new dawn of the early morning sunrise, comes only after the long day of absolute silence and darkness while the crucified victim remains in the tomb."[28] The Mexican people were in the midst of a historical night, the darkness and suffering of the Spanish conquest, a violence that not only spilled their blood and forced them into servitude, but also destroyed their cohesive

---

23. Elizondo, *Guadalupe*, 65.

24. Elizondo, "Mary and Evangelization," 157.

25. Elizondo, *Guadalupe*, 68–69. Hence, likewise, while Jeanette Rodriguez is correct to see the message of Guadalupe as concerning human relationships, one must be careful to avoid a formal reduction of God to a mere symbol of healthy relationships. See J. Rodriguez, "Theological Aesthetics and the Encounter with Tonantzin Guadalupe," 33. Love of God and love of neighbor are two unique and irreducible relationships that are nevertheless deeply interwoven and mutually intensifying. See Catherine of Siena, *Dialogue*, 121.

26. Elizondo, *Future Is Mestizo*, 59.

27. Elizondo, *Guadalupe*, 6, 25.

28. Ibid., xx.

religious view of the world, which had given meaning to their lives.[29] In response, the Guadalupe event represents the light of a new dawn. Early Christian Nahuatl songs and prayers associated Christ with the sun, and Mary, as his mother, represented the dawn with its transformational power. Louise Burkhart writes, "Mary, as mother of this solarized Christ, catalyzed the transformation of the familiar world into its sacred aspect as well as the transition from what was now seen as the 'darkness' of traditional religion into the light of Christianity."[30] Without justifying the darkness of violence, Elizondo points to a purpose that *cuts through* it. As Mary Doak points out, by placing the story of Guadalupe within the history of the conquest, the Guadalupe narrative *interrupts* and *reinterprets* history in light of hope.[31] Guadalupe brings hope to the darkness, and this hope is the breaking of dawn.

In Guadalupe, the biblical idea of God's creative power over primordial chaos, re-imagined through apocalyptic re-creation, merges with the Nahuatl concept of the world as a series of recurrent creations. Guadalupe becomes, at the herald of the fifth and final creation, the pronouncement of the eschatological age.[32] Although this marriage of indigenous and Christian categories occurred easily in view of Nahuatl apocalypticism, it poses a challenge. The Nahuas were able to conceptualize the divine, transcendent meaning of history because they tended toward a constitutively deterministic worldview, which threatened to reduce history to a mere shadow of the transcendent.[33] Even within Nahua thought, this kind of thinking put into question the possibility of encountering truth within an evanescent world.[34]

29. Ibid., 31.
30. Burkhart, "Cult of the Virgin of Guadalupe," 211–12.
31. Doak, *Reclaiming Narrative*, 191.
32. Elizondo, *Guadalupe*, 32–34. The Nahua believed that the world had been destroyed a number of times before, and humans remade each time. Although Elizondo refers to five ages or "suns," different historical sources actually disagree on the precise number. See also Harrington, "Mother of Death, Mother of Rebirth," 29.

León-Portilla notes that the Mexica enshrined "the concept of perpetual struggle for supremacy as a framework in which the occurrence of cosmic events can be understood." *Aztec Thought and Culture*, 48. In effect, the violent upheaval of apocalypse was formalized until it became prescriptive in the sacrificial cult. The periods between violent cataclysms represented mere ceasefires amidst the everlasting conflict between the gods.

33. This determinism stood in tension (and constant struggle) with the Huitzilopochtli cult, which allowed humans to delay the end of the sun through human sacrifice. See León-Portilla, *Aztec Image of Self and Society*, 101.

34. See ibid., 170–71.

In response, Christianity must interpose hope within the openness of the future, inasmuch as history is the location of the radical in-breaking of the divine.[35] This ultimately nourishes a tension between *a priori* and *a posteriori* meaning for history, and between the "already" of Christ's Incarnation, death, and Resurrection and the "not yet" of eschatological fulfillment.

Guadalupe is a "precipitate" event. Within the dark of the cosmic night, the long-awaited divine revelation comes unexpectedly, almost "too early," like flowers that are "out of season." It is the announcement of the "God of unexpected surprises."[36] At the same time, this event is "precipitated" by the work of Christ, as the logical outcome and pronouncement of the Gospel message.[37] Guadalupe orients history itself in relation to the coming of Christ. As Elizondo states, "For Guadalupe history is continuity with the past recycled into the new being of the future that begins in the present moment: the past and the future are alive in us."[38]

A New Revelation of Humanity

It is in this sense that Guadalupe constitutes a "new" revelation. It is not something new over and against the Gospel, but neither is it simply reducible to a mere restatement. Something distinctive is accomplished in Guadalupe that makes it an irreplaceable, constitutive part of the unfolding of salvation history. Guadalupe announces a new humanity by *embodying* it. She proclaims a humanity that finds itself in the forgotten and downtrodden other, the one whom society has rejected and victimized. As an eschatological proclamation of a new creation, Guadalupe is both the revelation of something new—an authentically new world—and of *newness itself*, the

---

35. Cf. Ashley, "Apocalypticism," 32–33. Ashley characterizes Metz's view thus: "It is the preunderstanding of time as a closed continuum, in which the future can be nothing more than the extrapolation of past and present, that paralyzes our imaginative sense for the new bursting out among us, that leaves us trapped in the failed ideologies and structures (be they liberal or conservative) of the past. The *apocalyptic* feeling for time, Metz contends, is one that hopes for, and thus is constantly on the look-out for, God's mighty deeds, breaking out in unexpected places and, like the resurrection, bringing life from death." This interplay of freedom and determinism is already operative in biblical apocalyptic. See Collins, *Apocalyptic Imagination*, 109.

36. Elizondo, "Mary and Evangelization," 152. Elizondo takes up this phrase from Raymond Brown.

37. See Elizondo, *Guadalupe*, 134–36.

38. Ibid., 117.

renovation of the political and social order after the pattern of the Kingdom of God.[39] "In spite of the threats of death, Guadalupe is an experience and guarantee of life."[40] Elizondo summarizes the eschatology of Guadalupe:

> At that unique moment in the history of our planet, God intervened to open up the possibilities for the eventual unity of all peoples. . . . We—Europeans and natives—wanted bloodshed and victims, but God wanted flower and songs. . . . Guadalupe, like Jesus, reverses the intent and purpose of the world by introducing a totally new creation, a totally new vision of the new humanity, a totally new way of bringing it about, a new cosmic order. She opens the way for a global universality that the world has never known: a universality of harmony, a universality of respect for others in their differences, a universality of love, compassion, and mutual aid. This is the ultimate order that we need to work to bring about.[41]

Guadalupe opens up the possibility of a reversal of injustice grounded in the rediscovery of a more fundamental, more transcendent *a priori*: the eschatological love of God. Against the determinism of sin, she recovers the freedom of hope.

SÁNCHEZ'S WOMAN OF THE APOCALYPSE

Without having explicitly defined an "apocalyptic school" of theology, we can nevertheless see that Elizondo's theology of Guadalupe deserves to be called "apocalyptic." Elizondo utilizes a distinctively "apocalyptic rhetoric," rendering historical events transparent to the saving action of God, and urging social praxis and responsibility in the face of the present dominion of sin.[42] Yet his apocalyptic is not merely a rhetorical device. It incorporates a holistic apocalyptic viewpoint inspired by a long (though not univocal) history of apocalyptic discourses. Miguel Sánchez's interpretation of the image in relation to Revelation 12 in *Imagen de la Virgen María* (1648)[43] stands as an important moment in that history.

39. See ibid., 129.
40. Elizondo, *Future Is Mestizo*, 66.
41. Elizondo, *Guadalupe*, 132–34.
42. See Ashley, "Apocalypticism," 25; O'Leary, *Arguing the Apocalypse*.
43. Sánchez, "Imagen de la Virgen María Madre de Dios de Guadalupe," 152–281. For an excellent summary of this text, see Brading, *Mexican Phoenix*, 54–75. A heavily

The Background of Sánchez's Account

Written in Spanish, primarily for educated clergy, Sánchez's *Imagen* contains the first published account of the Guadalupe apparition. By positioning the Guadalupe narrative within the wider semiotic matrix of Scripture, tradition, and the Fathers, Sánchez seeks to provide spiritual edification and inspirational material for preaching. At the time, his principle audience was American-born Spaniards, known as *criollos*. Jacques Lafaye has shown how Sánchez's account contributed to the formation of a unique *criollo* identity, in contradistinction to that of mainland Spain, by allowing them to understand themselves apocalyptically as a people uniquely chosen by Mary of Guadalupe.[44] Partly due to Sánchez's influential interpretation, Guadalupe successfully won the heart of the Mexican people, and became a symbol of independence, cultural identity, and political/social nationalism. For centuries after its publication, Sánchez's version of the apparition narrative—especially as abbreviated by Mateo de la Cruz—was more widely circulated than the *Nican mopohua*, and greatly influenced interpretations of the apparition and image.

In contrast, current scholarship grants almost exclusive focus to the *Nican mopohua* because of its peculiarly indigenous voice.[45] Inspired by Sánchez's account, the *criollo* priest Luis Laso de la Vega published the *Nican mopohua* in 1649, as part of a larger volume called the *Huei tlamahuiçoltica*. Although not entirely free from Spanish influence, the *Nican mopohua* utilizes Nahuatl idiom and categories, represents an indigenous viewpoint, and may even derive from an earlier oral tradition. Nevertheless, while it lacks Sánchez's biblical and patristic references, the *Nican mopohua* is basically similar to Sánchez's account. Both texts include the same themes, narrative elements, and role-reversal that scholars today interpret

---

abridged translation of Sánchez's apparition narrative and the miracle accounts, minus Sánchez's expressly theological observations, is available in Sousa et al., *Story of Guadalupe*, 131–45. Unless otherwise specified, quotes from Sánchez are my own, with reference to Sousa et al.

44. Lafaye, *Quetzalcóatl and Guadalupe*, 250; see Matovina, "Guadalupe at Calvary," 799–800. Sánchez's pro-*criollo* advocacy must be understood as *de facto*, and not as a kind of exclusivist lobbying. Hence there is no basis for suggesting, as David A. Sánchez does, that Miguel Sánchez intentionally wrote his *Imagen* so as to cover up and subvert its earlier, pro-indigenous meaning. This claim overlooks both the indigenous elements of Sánchez's narrative and the irreducibly Spanish elements of the *Nican mopohua*. Cf. Sánchez, *From Patmos to the Barrio*, 76.

45. See Brading's comments on José Luis Guerrero in *Mexican Phoenix*, 357.

as carrying liberative meaning. Accordingly, utilizing the *Nican mopohua*, theologians today locate the liberative message of the Guadalupe event within the context of salvation history, in much the same way as Sánchez himself. As Matovina notes, "Consciously or not . . . the current emphasis on the *Nican mopohua* employs Sánchez's central themes, albeit as reexamined from a liberationist perspective."[46]

Nevertheless, the *Imagen* has appropriately been criticized for portraying Our Lady of Guadalupe as the chief *conquistadora*, who legitimates violent subjugation of the New World.[47] This assertion must be taken with a grain of salt, keeping in mind the biases of Spanish Christians at the time, along with the exceptional struggles of figures like Bartolomé de las Casas, who fought for the lives, freedom, and dignity of indigenous Americans against such theological justifications of violence. The image of Our Lady of Guadalupe ultimately conquered the hearts of the subjugated indigenous Mexican people in a way that Spanish muskets and swords never could. She fought for the dignity of the people with flower and song.[48]

The Woman Clothed with the Sun

The basis of Sánchez's theological interpretation is his identification of the image of Guadalupe with the woman "clothed with the sun" in chapter 12 of the book of Revelation. This biblical link stems from the character of the image itself, which despite its indigenous traits, fits the characteristics of a traditional Christian portrayal of the Immaculate Conception of Mary in terms of Revelation 12.[49] This pictorial association of Mary with the biblical woman clothed in the sun was promoted by Quodvultdeus in the 5th century, in a sermon that until the 20th century carried the name and authority of Augustine.[50] In fact, it is likely that the name "Guadalupe" became

---

46. Matovina, "Guadalupe at Calvary," 809.
47. Sánchez, "Imagen," 179; Matovina, "Guadalupe at Calvary," 808.
48. Cf. Elizondo, *Guadalupe*, 6; Sánchez, "Imagen," 109.
49. Harrington, "Mother of Death, Mother of Rebirth" 36.
50. Matovina, "Guadalupe at Calvary," 801. Matovina explains, "It is worth noting that the association of the woman in Revelation 12 with Mary is quite rare among early Christian writers. Indeed, few patristic authors before the sixth century comment on the book of Revelation and those that do tend to link the woman in chapter 12 directly with the Church rather than Mary."

attributed to the image because of its resemblance to another such image in the choir at the basilica of Our Lady of Guadalupe in Extremadura, Spain.[51]

Even though the Joachimite expectations of the Spanish conquerors underlie his justification of the Spanish conquest, Sánchez's account communicates a genuinely apocalyptic perspective. As Matovina states, "Sánchez follows Augustine and other patristic theologians by exploring biblical narrative and imagery as the primal lens through which to interpret historical and contemporary events."[52] According to patristic biblical exegesis, Scripture passages communicate a broad plurality of meaning. This mindset allows Sánchez to understand Revelation 12 as genuinely speaking about Our Lady of Guadalupe without denying other historical interpretations of the text. For Sánchez's, St. John's "vision on Patmos of the Woman of the Apocalypse was now materially realized in the image of the New World."[53] This places the cosmic battle between Michael and the dragon in the context of the New World, as the struggle for the soul of Mexico.[54] For Sánchez, the Bible is no mere book about the past; it speaks about the present, the future, and the theological character of time itself.

The Prophetic Call

Revelation 12 belongs to a history of biblical and Near Eastern apocalyptic, which itself belongs to a broader history of prophetic literature exemplified in the Old Testament. Although not all biblical prophetic is explicitly apocalyptic, and not every apocalyptic vision in the Bible is interpreted by someone who is officially a "prophet," one cannot overlook the intimate connection in the Bible between prophethood and apocalyptic. As Sánchez points out, the Guadalupe apparition account explicitly casts Juan Diego into the role of a biblical prophet, specifically after the pattern of Moses.[55]

---

51. See Poole, *Our Lady of Guadalupe*, 74–75. The original feast day associated with the Mexican shrine was not December 12, but September 8, the feast of the Nativity of Mary, which was also the feast of the Extremaduran Guadalupe. Ibid., 51, 60; see also Lafaye, *Quetzalcóatl and Guadalupe*, 235.

52. Matovina, "Guadalupe at Calvary," 801.

53. Brading, *Mexican Phoenix*, 63; Sánchez, "Imagen," 191–92.

54. Sánchez, "Imagen," 176–77.

55. Ibid., 194.

apocalypse at tepeyac

In the Bible, a prophet is not a mere fortune-teller, one who professes to know the future.[56] A prophet pronounces God's Word to the people, whether it be a word of judgment or mercy, lamentation or consolation. The prophet is an authorized divine spokesperson, who receives a specific authority to speak through an event of commissioning that brings the prophet into "the historical line of continuity from the ancient mediators," especially Moses.[57] In this sense, one can speak of prophethood as an interplay of authority and the rejection of authority. The prophet refuses to speak for him or herself, but only strives to mediate the "The Word of the Lord," which "comes to" the prophet despite himself.

The event of the biblical prophet's commissioning, known as a "call narrative," carries a formal structure that enacts this play of authority. Its chief parts are as follows: (1) divine confrontation (2) introductory word (3) commissioning (4) the prophet's objection (5) divine reassurance and (6) a sign.[58] Examples of this format can be found throughout the Bible, although it is not representative of every single person referred to as a "prophet," nor is every element present in each call narrative. This format is, however, representative of the call of Juan Diego in both the *Imagen* and the *Nican mopohua*.

The *divine confrontation* (1) is a theophanous event where the prophet encounters the otherness of God in a way that tends to stress the dire situation in which God's Word is sent into the world. Moses encounters the voice of God in a burning bush that is not consumed (Exod 3:1–4a), Isaiah sees the Lord enthroned among the seraphim (Isa 6:1–2), Ezekiel is "among the exiles by the river Chebar" when "the heavens were opened, and I saw visions of God," the four "living creatures" and God's bizarre chariot (Ezek 1:1–28). These details provide some indication of the historical time or place where God suddenly intervenes in history. Against the background of the violent upheaval of the conquest, "one Saturday (the day had to be consecrated to Mary)," Juan Diego heard "sweet music" with perfect form, played by a heavenly band of angels.[59]

In many ways, the divine confrontation is already apocalyptic. It is a violent eruption of God within the world, "portrayed in a manner which tends to emphasize the disruptive and overwhelming character of the call

---

56. See Vawter, *Conscience of Israel*, 25f.
57. Habel, "Form and Significance of the Call Narratives," 316.
58. Ibid., 297–323.
59. Sánchez, "Imagen," 179; cf. Elizondo, *Guadalupe*, 6.

encounter which could not be readily described in terms of a normal everyday occurrence."[60] It may be experienced by the prophet as a situation of great distress, which will underline the mission on which he is about to be sent. Juan Diego pauses in bewilderment at the music, which is beyond even the beauty of bird-song. In the *Nican mopohua*, he wonders, "Maybe I am dreaming? Maybe I am in the land of my ancestors, of the elders, of our grandparents? Maybe over there inside of heaven?"[61]

The *introductory word* (2) "provides the necessary ground and background to the specific commission which is to follow," affirming the status of the personal relationship between God and the chosen individual.[62] By way of dialogue, God links the mission of the prophet with both the history of Israel and the prophet's own personal history. In the case of Moses, the Lord informs him that "I am the God of your father . . ." and "I have seen the affliction of my people" (Exod 3:7–8). The introductory words can also serve as an initial reassurance and empowerment: "Son of man, stand upon your feet, and I will speak with you" (Ezek 2:1). Similarly, Mary clears Juan's heart of fear: "Standing in her presence, astonished without fearing, bewildered without confusion, attentive without fright, he contemplated a beauty that inspired love without danger, a light that illuminated him without leaving him dazzled, an affability that captivated him without flattery."[63] She asks, "Son Juan, where are you going?"[64] Her question invites Juan to recognize the connection between what he is currently doing—going to Mass—and this chance encounter. Sánchez sees in her address of "Son" a reference to John the Apostle, to whom Jesus entrusted his mother at the foot of the cross.[65]

The *commissioning* (3) is a direct, personal imperative that sends the prophet on a specific mission. The command tends to involve more than merely repeating some divine statement. It is a mission that will encompass the prophet's entire life. Moses is sent to Pharaoh to bring forth God's people. Isaiah is sent to condemn the people with his words (Isa 6:9–13). "In each case it becomes apparent that the commission involves a range of activities

---

60. Habel, "Form and Significance," 317.

61. Elizondo, *Guadalupe*, 6–7.

62. Habel, "Form and Significance," 318.

63. Sousa et al., *Story of Guadalupe*, 131; Sánchez, "Imagen," 179; cf. Elizondo, *Guadalupe*, 7. This encounter is also reminiscent of Rev 1:9–20.

64. Sánchez, "Imagen," 179; Elizondo, *Guadalupe*, 7.

65. Sánchez, "Imagen," 179.

which is beyond the range of the individual's natural ability."[66] Juan Diego is sent to the bishop of Mexico to have him erect at Tepeyac a "home" (*casa/acatl*), a "chapel" (*ermita/teocaltzin*), a "temple" (*templo/teocalli*) for Mary.[67] Roberto Goizueta reflects on how Juan Diego's call restores his identity as a subject in the face of sinful oppression: "The Lady *chooses* him, his identity, and his mission; in so doing, she liberates him to *act* in history."[68]

The most important element linking Moses and Juan Diego is the *objection* (4). The true prophet professes his unworthiness and unsuitability for God's work. This is not merely a statement of personal humility, "but rather a part of his office as servant, mediator and agent of Yahweh."[69] Moses exclaims, "Who am I that I should go to Pharaoh, and bring the sons of Israel out of Egypt?" (Exod 3:11). Elsewhere, he insists that the Lord send someone else because "I am slow of speech and of tongue" (Exod 4:10).[70] Isaiah, afraid that for a sinner to see the Lord means certain death, cries out, "Woe is me! For I am lost; for I am a man of unclean lips" (Isa 6:5). Jeremiah objects that he is too young (Jer 1:6). Juan Diego's objection comes after his initial failure. He delivers Mary's message to the bishop, who listens but remains unconvinced, asking him to come back some other time.[71] He returns to Tepeyac and begs Mary's forgiveness, asking her to send someone else who will be more likely to be believed—essentially, a Spanish nobleman. "Because I am in reality one of those campesinos," he says in the *Nican mopohua*, "a piece of rope, a small ladder, the excrement of the people."[72] Because of the subjugation of the conquest and the oppressiveness of the enforced caste system, he has come to devalue himself, and is afraid of disappointing Mary. Unlike Isaiah, the Guadalupe accounts do not attribute sinfulness to Juan Diego. He merely *perceives* himself as unworthy because society has told him so. Juan is not

---

66. Habel, "Form and Significance," 318.

67. Sánchez, "Imagen," 180; Elizondo, *Guadalupe*, 8. The three terms are used explicitly in both the Spanish and Nahuatl accounts.

68. Goizueta, "Resurrection at Tepeyac," 343.

69. Habel, "Form and Significance," 319; see also Vawter, *Conscience of Israel*, 47–48.

70. Habel notes, "Behind Moses' exclamation of humility lies the history of Moses the murderer." Habel, "Form and Significance," 304. Moses failed to save his people before, and he feels powerless to save them still.

71. Contemporary dramatic representations of the apparition story sometimes exaggerate the bishop's rejection of Juan in order to draw a more stark contrast between the two. However, both seminal accounts describe the bishop as cordial and polite—far from a villain, but foolishly unable to recognize the truth of Juan's words without a sign.

72. Elizondo, *Guadalupe*, 10.

in need of personal moral purification, but of purification from the sins of others that have blinded him to his own worth.

The *reassurance* (5) repeats the divine call and forcefully overcomes the prophet's objections. Moses is assured, "I shall be with you" (Exod 3:12). Jeremiah is told not to worry about his youth: "Be not afraid of them, for I am with you to deliver you" (Jer 1:8). Guadalupe echoes Scripture's emphasis on the divine *I AM* by asking Juan to repeat to the bishop "firmly that I, Mary the Virgin Mother of God, am the one who has sent you."[73]

The concluding *sign* (6) provides a confirmation of the mission and provides the prophet with the credentials for carrying out the task at hand. It may be directed toward the recipients of God's message or toward the prophet himself. God touches Jeremiah's mouth, enabling him to speak God's Word. Even more dramatically, Ezekiel is given a scroll to eat. In response to Isaiah's protestation of sin, an angel presses a burning coal to Isaiah's lips, cleansing him. Moses is given two signs. For his own confirmation he is given a deferred promise: "when you have brought forth the people out of Egypt, you shall serve God upon this mountain" (Exod 3:12). For the people, he is told to say, "I AM has sent me to you" (Exod 3:14). Juan Diego receives three signs. For himself, he receives the miraculous healing of his uncle, Juan Bernardino.[74] For the bishop, he receives the miraculous flowers on top of the hill.[75] The final and definitive sign comes as a surprise. When Juan meets with the bishop and opens his cloak to reveal the flowers, the miraculous image of Guadalupe suddenly appears on the cloth of his garment.[76]

By exemplifying the characteristics of the prophetic call narrative, the Guadalupe apparition narrative thus identifies Juan Diego as a prophet in dynamic continuity with Moses. His prophetic role is enacted in the dramatic sign-act of going forth on his mission. In this way, the commissioning itself is proclaimed as the very Word of God: those who have been rejected, downtrodden, cast aside by the world are chosen by God to carry out the Gospel. Mary freely admits that she could have chosen many others who were better qualified for the mission, whom the bishop would have listened to. Still she tells Juan, "But it is absolutely necessary that you personally go and speak about this, and that precisely through your mediation and help,

---

73. Sánchez, "Imagen," 182; cf. Elizondo, *Guadalupe*, 11; see Habel, "Form and Significance," 309.

74. Sánchez, "Imagen," 186; Elizondo, *Guadalupe*, 14–16.

75. Sánchez, "Imagen," 187; Elizondo, *Guadalupe*, 16–17.

76. Sánchez, "Imagen," 190–91; Elizondo, *Guadalupe*, 20.

apocalypse at tepeyac

my wish and my desire be revealed."[77] In effect, the mediation (Juan Diego) becomes part of the very content of revelation itself.

The Interpreter of Revelation

This point leads us to the specifically *apocalyptic* character of Juan Diego's role. The biblical genre of apocalyptic insists that revelation is best given not in simple propositional statements, but by means of an *interpreter* who is transparent to divine revelation. In view of the apocalyptic visions of Ezekiel and Daniel, and Joseph's interpretation of dreams, the necessity of interpretation is not an unfortunate corruption of revelation, but part of the very character of revelation itself, which in its gratuitous openness defies the reductive limitations of human knowledge.[78] Biblical apocalyptic communicates the divine word in fantastic and theophanous categories because these lend themselves to a plurality of meaning that can only be brought forth by means of the specially authorized interpreter—the one who reads the vision *in the Spirit*.

The book of Daniel is a key example. Throughout the book there are repeated examples of vivid, pictorial visions, which require an interpreter in order to be understood. Twice, Daniel is called upon to interpret the dreams of King Nebuchadnezzar (Dan 2:1–45; 4:1–27). Only Daniel can unlock the secrets of these dreams, sent by God, "for the spirit of the holy gods is in you" (Dan 4:18). Accordingly, "The dream is certain, and its interpretation sure" (Dan 2:45). Daniel likewise interprets the mysterious writing on the wall for King Belshazzar (Dan 5:5–30). Eventually, the book moves on to a dream and two visions granted to Daniel himself and interpreted by an angel (Dan 7:1–28; 8:1–27; 10:1–12:13).[79] Only in the earlier events is Daniel the principle interpreter, but for all of the visions he is the main perspective character. One way or another, he mediates the revelation. Details about the prophet's life and the situation in which the vision arrives serve to accentuate the specifically historical relevance of apocalyptic as the *in-breaking* of divine revelation into the finitude of time and place.[80]

---

77. Elizondo, *Guadalupe*, 10; cf. Sánchez, "Imagen," 182; Sousa et al., *Story of Guadalupe*, 121.

78. See Collins, *Apocalyptic Imagination*, 107–8.

79. The first two visions name Gabriel as the interpreter.

80. It is interesting, then, that postbiblical Daniel apocalypses and apocalyptic oracles tend to do away with those elements that stress the spatial and temporal coordinates of the revelation. DiTommaso, "Early Christian Daniel Apocalyptica," 231–32.

In the same way, Juan Diego is the perspective character for the Guadalupe apparition narratives. Sánchez sees him as a type of John of Patmos, to whom the risen Jesus appears in the book of Revelation.[81] John witnesses remarkable events in the heavenly court, explained variously by Jesus, a voice, an angel, or an elder. The prophetic interplay of authority and the rejection of authority is stressed here. John is a privileged witness because of his unique personal experience, even though his understanding of such is supernaturally mediated through an interpreter. In effect, the apocalyptic prophet is specially endowed with a mission and divine authorization for mediating this revelation to others, even though he can claim nothing of his own. Far from a neutral observer, the apocalyptic witness becomes an interpreter in his own right.[82] Yet he is not chosen because of any innate fittingness for the job. Rather, as shown in the case of Juan Diego, God addresses "the least of these" as privileged vehicles of God's own historical self-communication. This option for the lowly belongs properly to revelation itself, such that there can be no demythologization that separates out the raw content of revelation from its mode of communication in the poor, the outcast, and the rejected. As Elizondo states, "What human beings reject, God chooses as his very own."[83]

In the ancient world the hill or mountain was a place (τόπος) of the encounter with the divine. This was no different in the Nahua mindset, which formalized this τόπος in the construction of pyramids.[84] Moses encountered the Lord on Horeb (Exod 3:1); John of Patmos saw the Lamb atop Mount Zion (Rev 14:1); Juan Diego found the Queen of Heaven on the hill of Tepeyac.[85] Sánchez sees Tepeyac as a "new Tabor," recalling the mountain where Christ was transfigured in the Gospel accounts.[86] Likewise, Juan Diego's trip atop the mountain to collect flowers is compared to Moses's third ascent of Mount Sinai. Moses was instructed in the care of the Ark of the Covenant, while Juan Diego goes in service of Mary, the

---

81. Sánchez, "Imagen," 160, 179. Like John, Juan Diego is given a message for a particular church (Rev 2–3).

82. See Collins, *Apocalyptic Imagination*, 282–83.

83. Elizondo, *Galilean Journey*, 92.

84. J. Rodriguez, *Our Lady of Guadalupe*, 49.

85. On the significance of mountains in early Christian apocalyptic images, see Herrmann and van der Hoek, "Apocalyptic Themes in the Monumental and Minor Art of Early Christianity," 36–44.

86. Sánchez, "Imagen," 184.

apocalypse at tepeyac

"true Ark."[87] Tepeyac's flowers are described as a "spring of heaven" and "garden of paradise," recalling the return of the Garden of Eden as a symbol of eschatological harmony and fulfillment.[88] Elizondo adds that Tepeyac "is the Mount of the Beatitudes of the Americas," where "we can hear and experience a blessing pronounced on the poor, the meek, the lowly, the sorrowing, the peacemakers, and the persecuted of the New World." [89]

As an eschatological-apocalyptic encounter, Tepeyac implicitly becomes a counter-symbol of the hill of apocalyptic violence, *Har Megiddo*, from which comes the word Armageddon (Rev 16:16).[90] For Sánchez, Guadalupe is a sign that the violent struggle between Michael and the dragon is at an end.[91] While he too easily associates the victory of Guadalupe with the violence of the Spanish conquerors, his primary characterization of the intervention of Guadalupe is not in terms of *la conquistadora*. Rather, for Sánchez, Our Lady of Guadalupe represents a paradisiacal refuge, a new Eden without the flaming swords of the Cherubim.[92] The apocalypse of Guadalupe signifies the cessation of violence and the definitive return of peace. As Elizondo writes, "Guadalupe, like Jesus, reverses the intent and purpose of the world by introducing a totally new creation, a totally new vision of the new humanity, a totally new way of bringing it about, a new cosmic order."[93]

The formal structure of the story of Guadalupe thus recalls that of biblical apocalyptic. Yet it is also follows traditional patterns characteristic of Christian "finding" narratives. These accounts are especially rooted in the Spanish experience of Moorish domination in the eighth century.[94] Under Islamic rule, many Christian sanctuaries were dismantled or taken over, and images were destroyed by Islamic iconoclasm. After the Christian reconquest of Spain, hagiographical accounts proliferated wherein lowly but blessed individuals miraculously rediscovered lost images that had been hidden away for safety. The story of the Extremaduran image of Our Lady of Guadalupe

---

87. Ibid., 185–86.
88. Ibid., 187; cf. Burkhart, "Cult of the Virgin of Guadalupe," 210–11.
89. Elizondo, *Guadalupe*, 47.
90. Armageddon is the symbol of the apocalypse-as-violence, both in terms of divine judgment and human self-annihilation.
91. Cf. Harrington, "Mother of Death, Mother of Rebirth," 38.
92. Sánchez, "Imagen," 233; 180, 227, 259.
93. Elizondo, *Guadalupe*, 132–34.
94. See Harrington, "Mother of Death, Mother of Rebirth," 28.

exemplifies this kind of narrative.[95] This style of inspirational story was quickly imported to the New World.[96] The protagonists of such tales would have been perceived as lowly because of their indigenous or African blood.[97]

Guadalupe roughly follows this pattern while expanding upon it by incorporating an interplay of the old and the new, rediscovery and invention.[98] The image that Juan Diego uncovers is not one that was previously hidden away, but something strikingly new—an image believed to have been divinely painted.[99] The image, like Revelation 12 itself and the dreams interpreted by Daniel and Joseph, bears an artistic depth that invites a wealth of interpretation. In this way, the Guadalupe account affirms an unusual coherence between the narrative and the image. The image is not incidental to the apparition account, but proclaims it in its own pictorial way. The apocalyptic encounter with Guadalupe continues in the relationship between the icon and the viewer. It invites us to become new witnesses to an ongoing revelation, for which the voice of the poor serves as the privileged source of interpretation.

Sánchez himself plays a part in the ongoing unfolding of revelation through interpretation. Elizondo writes, "Certain persons are able to play key roles in the recording and shaping of history by interpreting the past in such a way that it becomes a dynamic force which will determine the future. Father Miguel Sánchez was such a person."[100] Sánchez likens himself to an artist attempting to replicate a beautiful painting. "I have set myself up as the painter of that holy image by writing about it," writes Sánchez, "I have put all possible vigilance into copying it; love of the fatherland in describing it; Christian wonder in painting it; I shall also put diligence into the fine details."[101] Yet he

95. Brading, *Mexican Phoenix*, 36–37; Poole, *Our Lady of Guadalupe*, 23–24.

96. E.g. *Nuestra Señora de los Remedios* and *Nuestra Señora de la Caridad del Cobre*. Poole, *Our Lady of Guadalupe*, 24.

97. Of course, Lafaye sees no transcendent meaning in the indigenous protagonist of the Guadalupe story. Rather, it was part of a plot hatched to keep alms in the New World. Lafaye, *Quetzalcóatl and Guadalupe*, 235.

98. It is nevertheless misleading to characterize the similarity between Sánchez's Guadalupe narrative and the Extremaduran finding narrative as a *criollo* "subversion" or "mimicry" of a Spanish myth of power and oppression: cf. Sánchez, *From Patmos to the Barrio*, 71, 117.

99. Cf. the comparison between God and Praxiteles in Angel Betancurt's poem "Historia de la Milagrosa Imagen de Nuestra Señora de los Remedios": Poole, *Our Lady of Guadalupe*, 96–97.

100. Elizondo, *La Morenita*, 105.

101. Sánchez, "Imagen," 197.

apocalypse at tepeyac

finds himself no more able to express the depth of Our Lady of Guadalupe than the Greek painter Apelles was able to capture the beauty of Helen.[102] The task of the interpreter always extends beyond the limits of human τέχνη. This does not mean that the role of the interpreter in mediating revelation can be bypassed or ignored. We are called to receive God's Word mediated by the poor, and to become mediations for others.

GUADALUPE AND THE MEMORY OF SUFFERING

These analyses of the Guadalupe apparition narratives have revealed the apocalyptic character of Guadalupe's message especially along three distinct axes. In terms of its formal presentation, the Guadalupe narrative borrows important elements from biblical prophetic and apocalyptic literature in order to express the Guadalupe event as an important continuation of the critical history of God's salvation. At the same time, this format enacts a theological perspective on divine revelation wherein God's Word is best understood in and through the critical stance of the interpreter, who opens up the depth of God's self-communication by reading concrete revelation "in the Spirit." This stance is irreducibly counter-objective, non-neutral, and thus refuses to stand aside in the face of the experience of suffering in the world. As Collins notes, "apocalyptic language is *commissive* in character: it commits us to a view of the world for the sake of the actions and attitudes that are entailed."[103] Finally, Our Lady of Guadalupe presents a conception of finite history as the unique site of enactment of the divine plan of salvation.[104] It thus embodies the divine call for all people to take up the cause of the downtrodden, the vanquished, in order to become—as organs of the one body, the universal Church—real agents of the eschatological accomplishment of liberation.[105] Mary Doak explains, "In this view,

---

102. Ibid., 200–201.
103. Collins, *Apocalyptic Imagination*, 283.
104. Cf. Metz, *Faith in History and Society*, 109–10.

105. We have specifically avoided any attempt to construct an *eschatology* of Our Lady of Guadalupe. Although this would be a worthy task, inasmuch as apocalyptic and eschatology cannot be wholly separated, it nevertheless extends beyond the limits of a basic introduction to the apocalyptic character of the Guadalupe event. For without delineating the precise content of the concept of the eschatological future, we can still recognize, in view of the apocalyptic theology that we have introduced here, that the specifically apocalyptic character of this theology is its openness to the eschatological character of history and the future as such, in view of which the apocalypse is the scandalous

the salvation offered by God is not intended only for an afterlife in heaven but is part of God's will for this world: what will be accomplished beyond history begins and grows within history."[106]

These claims, however, rest upon the belief that Guadalupe was not "just another" Marian apparition, not a mere repeatable event within salvation history.[107] Christianity, in the Resurrection, is the belief that *something definitively new* is breaking out and has broken out within history that subverts the endless, repressive cycle of "nothing new under the sun" that perpetuates Nietzsche's "endless return of the same." In view of this, the theology of Guadalupe has to come to terms with the painful facts of history. How could the Guadalupe event have been an apocalyptic proclamation of the liberation of God when it has been followed by a long history of violence, suffering, and victimization?

The answer must lie, first and foremost, in the continuing validity of Guadalupe's message. Setting aside the existence of real and sometimes problematic co-determinants, wherein the Guadalupe image is venerated merely as a symbol of cultural identity, Mexican nationalism, or filial inheritance, we nevertheless find that the veneration of Our Lady of Guadalupe is growing stronger even today. Her help is sought out across the entire world in prayer and devotions. Her image has adorned campaigns for political justice.[108] Her face has inspired a new generation of artists and writers as they tackle problems of identity and history.[109] The enduring content of Guadalupe's message cannot be summed up in a single proposition. Nevertheless, this lasting faith-filled commitment to the Virgin of Guadalupe is underlined by the belief that one way or another, Guadalupe represents both a promise fulfilled and hopeful expectation of fulfillment to come. Political action underneath the banner of Guadalupe, the U.S. Latino theology of Virgilio Elizondo, and the apocalyptic theology of Miguel Sánchez share one element in particular: the conviction that the future promised in Guadalupe extends beyond the individual level, bearing groundbreaking ramifications for the political order.[110]

---

aletheia in history of God as the inner, transcendent meaning of the world. Cf. ibid., 112; Solovyov, *God, Man and the Church*, 49.

106. Doak, *Reclaiming Narrative*, 194.
107. Elizondo, *La Morenita*, 106; Goizueta, "Resurrection at Tepeyac," 337.
108. See, for example, Gálvez, *Guadalupe in New York*.
109. See, for example, Davalos, *Yolanda M. López*.
110. See Doak, *Reclaiming Narrative*, 194–97.

In this way, the apocalyptic theology of Guadalupe is not far removed from other contemporary apocalyptic approaches to theology. In particular, we can trace brief but important links to the thought of René Girard and Johann Baptist Metz.

René Girard

Girard's apocalyptic thought, most vividly expressed in his book *Battling to the End* (2007), revolves around his reading of Blaise Pascal's conflict between violence and truth.[111] This conflict is violently enshrined in history within the political structure, which has been a mere extension of the society's tendency to create peace through the bloody sacrifice of victims—the scapegoating mechanism. God has progressively revealed the truth about society's complicity in violence through the Scriptures. Christ's Incarnation, death, and Resurrection provide the definitive revelation of the scapegoating mechanism, as Christ's innocence proclaims the innocence of all victims, and that *"God is now on the side of the victim."*[112]

In effect, violence has outdone itself and begun a catastrophic meltdown. Because of Christ and Christianity, the old sacrifices of 'primitive' religion and society can no longer function as they once did. Nevertheless, their violence has continued to be enshrined within the political order, which has tried but failed to contain the apocalyptic escalation of violence through the ideology of heroism and the eroding laws of the "gentlemen's war."[113] The growing inability for the *politik* to control war has revealed the bitter truth: politics is war by other means.[114] The utopic vision of a technological society made 'good' by politics—which Metz calls the "teleological-technological concept of the future"—can no longer determine the meaning of the history of the world.[115]

The violence woven into the fabric of the political order and the liberating truth of the Gospel are at war with one another. Just as violence cannot destroy the truth, truth cannot extinguish violence violently. "All the lights of truth cannot arrest violence, and only serve to exasperate it."[116]

---

111. Girard, *Battling to the End*, 73, 80–81.
112. Ibid., xiv, 50, 114; see Girard, *Things Hidden*, 149, 208–9.
113. Girard, *Battling to the End*, 14, 66–69, 99.
114. See ibid., 221 n. 32; 109.
115. Metz, *Faith in History and Society*, 97.
116. Pascal, *Provincial Letters*, 336; cf. Elizondo, *Guadalupe*, 75.

New Frontiers in Guadalupan Studies

Truth and violence are growing side by side: "Our world is both the worst it has ever been, and the best."[117] Truth *destabilizes* violence, accelerating its eventual collapse. From the viewpoint of faith, although violence has its course to run, truth will prevail in the end.[118] Mary Doak's reflections on Guadalupe echo this perspective: "Despite all appearances to the contrary, life and love will survive and finally flourish; the self-aggrandizing and other-consuming power that is so often successful in this world will not achieve its end, but will consume itself. The dragon cannot win. We are called to share Mary's trust that God will save the vulnerable life that we cannot secure with our own powers."[119]

However, this also means that violence intensifies as it enters into its death-throes.[120] The towering edifice is crumbling above us. The question is, will we allow it to fall on our heads? For Girard, apart from faith, the triumph of truth over violence is far from certain, as people refuse to see what Christ has revealed.[121] The apocalyptic tension grows as humanity faces the realization that, because of the progress of technology, we are really capable of being the authors of our own extinction.[122] In response, "we have to wake up our sleeping consciences."[123] Renouncing violence, we have to abandon false attempts at consolation, at explaining away violence, at pretending that violence can bring about definitive peace.[124] Girard recommends the imitation of Christ as the only viable response to the destructive mimetic momentum of the world[125]—but this is a hope that fights through the dark of hopelessness, a discipleship that struggles to proclaim the Gospel amidst the growing tension of a world that escalates in violence.[126]

Likewise, Our Lady of Guadalupe contributes to the accelerating function of truth. Certainly racism, prejudice, violence, and subjugation continued after the apparition event. Yet this apparition has planted a seed

---

117. Girard, *Battling to the End*, 130; cf. *Girard Reader*, 274.

118. Girard, *Battling to the End*, 111; cf. Elizondo, "Bicultural Approach," 259.

119. Doak, "Facing the Dragon's Fire," 5.

120. Girard, *Battling to the End*, x–xi. This is because the revelation of the Gospel has depotentiated the scapegoat mechanism and all other attempts to contain violence, which used to provide *temporary* relief from the escalation to extremes. Ibid., xiv, 20.

121. Girard, *Battling to the End*, 81, 216–17.

122. Ibid., xiv, 217.

123. Ibid., 217.

124. Ibid., 46, 132.

125. Ibid., 102, 123.

126. See ibid., xiii.

of truth that resists the ongoing dominance of violence. More and more, we have come to recognize how the violence of the Spanish conquest, despite the good that eventually came out of it, was contrary to the truth of the Gospel. Moving away from Sánchez's validation of the conquest, contemporary theology has come to see how Guadalupe sides with the victims. Through her, we are beginning to understand, with Girard, how "Sin consists in thinking that something good could come from violence."[127] Doak writes, "Our Lady of Guadalupe makes herself vulnerable and takes the part of the vulnerable in the face of overwhelming opposition because she knows well that her task is not to stand on the side of the forces of self-serving power and this-worldly greatness that threaten life, but rather to nurture life against the odds, where it is most in danger from the dragons that would destroy it."[128]

Johann Baptist Metz

This function of Guadalupe can be further illuminated by recognizing her as a bearer of Metz's *memoria passionis*. Metz understands the history of Christ's passion and Resurrection as a recollection in solidarity of the ongoing history of the suffering of all victims. This "memory" is no mere intellectual acknowledgement of the sins of the past. Rather, as a "dangerous" memory, it engages in active critique of the violence inscribed in political structures today. Apocalyptically driven by the eschatological future of divine liberation, it "badgers the present and calls it into question, since it does not remember just any open future, but precisely this future, and because it compels believers to be in a continual state of transformation in order to take this future into account."[129]

In this way, the apocalyptic *novum* of Guadalupe is ironically delivered as a *reminder* to Bishop Juan de Zumárraga that his evangelical office must be carried out in solidarity with the poor. By proclaiming God's love for the indigenous poor, Guadalupe breaks the *memoria* of the Gospel out of the oppressive, relative confines into which it had been compressed. This message undoes the dehumanization of the conquest by announcing uncontrovertibly that yes, Jesus died for the people of the New World, too.

---

127. Girard, *Battling to the End*, 106; see also 44.
128. Doak, "Facing the Dragon's Fire," 3.
129. Metz, *Faith in History and Society*, 89.

Importantly, this *memoria* includes along with recognition of God's saving deeds in history also the irreconcilable prompting of the history of suffering within the world—a painful memory which, for Metz, cannot be dismissed. No evolutionary conclusion can simply justify the evil of suffering as a mere necessary consequence of a greater dialectical resolution for world history. The murdered victim can never be reduced to collateral damage.

Nevertheless, oppressive political structures frequently attempt to undermine the critical resistance of memory by erasing the past. The victor rewrites history in order to bind all memory to his own point of view. Aggression is rewritten as self-defense; violent annexation is framed as a legitimate purchase; forced conversion is called evangelization. The Nahuatl people underwent just such an event prior to the Spanish conquest, when the Mexica tribe rose to power and established themselves—despite their foreign origin—as the successors of the Toltec legacy. The leaders of the Mexica tribe enshrined this artificial history by forcibly burning historical books.[130] This act of rewriting history served to ground the violent political order of the Huitzilopochtli cult, which blatantly linked war, politics, and religion by carrying out bloody campaigns against neighboring tribes in order to procure a steady flow of sacrificial victims.[131]

Despite the efforts of various Spanish missionaries to understand the people of the New World and preserve their culture while presenting them with the truth, the rise of Spanish dominance proved itself to be much like that of the Mexica. The erasure of indigenous history and consequent denial to them of a voice was an attempt to hide the history of their suffering at the hands of the Spanish conquerors. It robbed them of a worldview and led them, like Juan Diego, to think of themselves as "a rope, a small ladder."

Guadalupe is the irruption of the divine *memoria passionis* in history in order to subvert this erasure and restore a history and a voice to a bloodied and disenfranchised people. The indigenous face of Guadalupe, by which she taps into pre-Hispanic culture and religion, restores the unique identity and history of the people before the conquest. "The lady hides *the sun* but does not extinguish it. . . . This is the assurance that their ancient way of life will continue, but now reinterpreted through something new and greater."[132] At the same time, she connects them quasi-sacramentally

---

130. León-Portilla, *Aztec Thought and Culture*, 155; *Aztec Image of Self and Society*, 79, 100.

131. León-Portilla, *Aztec Image of Self and Society*, 36.

132. Elizondo, *Future Is Mestizo*, 63.

to the wider history of the world's salvation in Jesus Christ. "In her, there is life, continuity, and transcendence; and most of all, there is hope for salvation here and now, today."[133] To the lowly recipients of Guadalupe's message no longer belongs merely *a* history, but *the* history, as their suffering comes to be understood in view of the wounds of Christ—for the apocalyptic message of Guadalupe insists that the history of the people of the New World is now irrevocably a part of the history of the saving work of Jesus Christ.

BIBLIOGRAPHY

Ashley, J. Matthew. "Apocalypticism in Political and Liberation Theology." *Horizons* 27.1 (2000) 22–43.

Brading, D. A. *Mexican Phoenix: Our Lady of Guadalupe; Image and Tradition across Five Centuries.* Cambridge: Cambridge University Press, 2001.

Burkhart, Louise M. "The Cult of the Virgin of Guadalupe in Mexico." In *South and Meso-American Native Spirituality: From the Cult of the Feathered Serpent to the Theology of Liberation*, edited by Gary H. Gossen and Miguel León-Portilla, 198–227. World Spirituality 4. New York: Crossroad, 1993.

Catherine of Siena. *The Dialogue.* Translated by Suzanne Noffke. The Classics of Western Spirituality. New York: Paulist, 1980.

Collins, John J. *The Apocalyptic Imagination: An Introduction to Jewish Apocalyptic Literature.* 2nd ed. Grand Rapids: William B. Eerdmans, 1998.

Davalos, Karen Mary. *Yolanda M. López.* A Ver: Revisioning Art History 2. Los Angeles: UCLA Chicano Studies Research Center Press, 2008.

DiTommaso, Lorenzo. "The Early Christian Daniel Apocalyptica." In *Apocalyptic Thought in Early Christianity*, edited by Robert J. Daly, 227–39. Holy Cross Studies in Patristic Theology and History. Grand Rapids: Baker Academic, 2009.

Doak, Mary. "Facing the Dragon's Fire." In *The Treasure of Guadalupe*, edited by Virgilio Elizondo, Allan Figueroa Deck, and Timothy M. Matovina, 1–8. Celebrating Faith. Lanham, MD: Rowman and Littlefield, 2006.

———. *Reclaiming Narrative for Public Theology.* SUNY Series, Religion and American Public Life. Albany: State University of New York Press, 2004.

Elizondo, Virgilio. "A Bicultural Approach to Religious Education." *Religious Education* 76.3 (1981) 258–70.

———. "Converted by Beauty." In *The Treasure of Guadalupe*, edited by Virgilio Elizondo, Allan Figueroa Deck, and Timothy M. Matovina, 73–78. Celebrating Faith. Lanham, MD: Rowman and Littlefield, 2006.

———. *The Future Is Mestizo: Life Where Cultures Meet.* Rev. ed. Boulder, CO: University Press of Colorado, 2000.

———. *Galilean Journey: The Mexican-American Promise.* Maryknoll, NY: Orbis, 1983.

———. *Guadalupe: Mother of the New Creation.* Maryknoll, NY: Orbis, 1997.

133. Elizondo, *Guadalupe*, 78.

New Frontiers in Guadalupan Studies

———. *La Morenita: Evangelizer of the Americas.* San Antonio: Mexican American Cultural Center, 1980.

———. "Mary and Evangelization in the Americas." In *Mary, Woman of Nazareth: Biblical and Theological Perspectives,* edited by Doris Donnelly, 146–60. New York: Paulist, 1989.

———. *Virgilio Elizondo: Spiritual Writings.* Edited by Timothy M. Matovina. Modern Spiritual Masters Series. Maryknoll, NY: Orbis, 2010.

Espín, Orlando O. *The Faith of the People: Theological Reflections on Popular Catholicism.* Maryknoll, NY: Orbis, 1997.

Gálvez, Alyshia. *Guadalupe in New York: Devotion and the Struggle for Citizenship Rights among Mexican Immigrants.* New York: New York University Press, 2010.

García-Rivera, Alejandro. "Crossing Theological Borders: Virgilio Elizondo's Place among Theologians of Culture." In *Beyond Borders: Writings of Virgilio Elizondo and Friends,* edited by Timothy M. Matovina, 246–56. Maryknoll, NY: Orbis, 2000.

Girard, René. *Battling to the End: Conversations with Benoît Chantre.* Translated by Mary Baker. Studies in Violence, Mimesis, and Culture. East Lansing: Michigan State University Press, 2010.

———. *The Girard Reader.* Edited by James G. Williams. New York: Crossroad, 1996.

———. *Things Hidden Since the Foundation of the World.* Translated by Stephen Bann and Michael Metteer. Stanford: Stanford University Press, 1987.

Goizueta, Roberto S. *Christ Our Companion: Toward a Theological Aesthetics of Liberation.* Maryknoll, NY: Orbis, 2009.

———. "Resurrection at Tepeyac: The Guadalupan Encounter." *Theology Today* 56.3 (1999) 336–345.

Habel, Norman C. "Form and Significance of the Call Narratives." *Zeitschrift für die alttestamentliche Wissenschaft* 77.3 (1965) 297–323.

Harrington, Patricia. "Mother of Death, Mother of Rebirth: The Mexican Virgin of Guadalupe." *Journal of the American Academy of Religion* 56.1 (1988) 25–50.

Herrmann, John, and Annewies van der Hoek. "Apocalyptic Themes in the Monumental and Minor Art of Early Christianity." In *Apocalyptic Thought in Early Christianity,* edited by Robert J. Daly, 33–80. Holy Cross Studies in Patristic Theology and History. Grand Rapids: Baker Academic, 2009.

Lafaye, Jacques. *Quetzalcóatl and Guadalupe: The Formation of Mexican National Consciousness, 1531–1813.* Translated by Benjamin Keen. Chicago: University of Chicago Press, 1976.

León-Portilla, Miguel. *The Aztec Image of Self and Society: An Introduction to Nahua Culture.* Translated by José Jorge Klor de Alva. Salt Lake City: University of Utah Press, 1992.

———. *Aztec Thought and Culture: A Study of the Ancient Nahuatl Mind.* Translated by Jack Emory Davis. Civilization of the American Indian Series 67. Norman: University of Oklahoma Press, 1990.

Matovina, Timothy M. "Guadalupe at Calvary: Patristic Theology in Miguel Sánchez's 'Imagen De La Virgen María' (1648)." *Theological Studies* 64 (2003) 795–811.

Metz, Johannes Baptist. *Faith in History and Society: Toward a Practical Fundamental Theology.* New York: Crossroad, 2007.

O'Leary, Stephen D. *Arguing the Apocalypse: A Theory of Millennial Rhetoric.* New York: Oxford University Press, 1998.

Pascal, Blaise. *The Provincial Letters of Blaise Pascal*. Translated by Orlando Williams Wight. Boston: Houghton, Osgood, 1880.
Poole, Stafford. *Our Lady of Guadalupe: The Origins and Sources of a Mexican National Symbol, 1531–1797*. Tucson: University of Arizona Press, 1995.
Rodriguez, Jeanette. "The Common Womb of the Americas: Virgilio Elizondo's Theological Reflection on Our Lady of Guadalupe." In *Beyond Borders: Writings of Virgilio Elizondo and Friends*, edited by Timothy M. Matovina, 109–17. Maryknoll, NY: Orbis Books, 2000.
———. *Our Lady of Guadalupe: Faith and Empowerment among Mexican-American Women*. Austin: University of Texas Press, 1994.
———. "Theological Aesthetics and the Encounter with Tonantzin Guadalupe." In *She Who Imagines: Feminist Theological Aesthetics*, edited by Laurie M. Cassidy and Maureen H. O'Connell, 17–34. Collegeville, MN: Liturgical, 2012.
Rodríguez, Rubén Rosario. "Beyond Word and Sacrament: A Reformed Protestant Engagement of Guadalupan Devotion." In *American Magnificat: Protestants on Mary of Guadalupe*, edited by Maxwell E. Johnson, 77–105. Collegeville, MN: Liturgical, 2010.
Sánchez, David A. *From Patmos to the Barrio: Subverting Imperial Myths*. Minneapolis: Fortress, 2008.
Sánchez, Miguel. "Imagen de la Virgen María Madre de Dios de Guadalupe." In *Testimonios históricos guadalupanos*, edited by Ernesto de la Torre Villar and Ramiro Navarro de Anda, 152–281. Sección de obras de historia. México: Fondo de Cultura Económica, 1982.
Siller Acuña, Clodomiro. *Flor Y Canto Del Tepeyac: Historia de Las Apariciones de Santa Maria de Guadalupe, Texto Y Comentario*. Xalapa, Veracruz, México: Servir, 1981.
Solovyov, Vladimir. *God, Man and the Church: The Spiritual Foundations of Life*. Translated by Donald Attwater. London: James Clarke, 1930.
Sousa, Lisa, Stafford Poole, and James Lockhart, eds. and trans. *The Story of Guadalupe: Luis Laso de la Vega's* Huei tlamahuiçoltica *of 1649*. Stanford: Stanford University Press, 1998.
Teilhard de Chardin, Pierre. *Hymn of the Universe*. Translated by Gerald Vann. New York: Harper & Row, 1965.
Vawter, Bruce. *The Conscience of Israel: Pre-Exilic Prophets and Prophecy*. New York: Sheed & Ward, 1961.

Index

Altamirano, Ignacio Manuel, 111, 112n12
Anderson, Arthur J. O., 20
Anunciación, Fray Domingo de la, 29
Apocalypse, 125–51, 126n4
Arteaga y Alfaro, Matías de, 57
Augustine, 135–36
Ave Maria, 19–20, 26, 28–29, 31–33, 36, 70
Baptism, 69–70, 69n9
Bargellini, Clara, 42
Basilicas of Our Lady of Guadalupe, 42, 46, 57, 136
Bautista, Fray Juan, 30–31
Becerra Tanco, Luis, 45, 57–58
Berceo, Gonzalo de, 79n33
Berndt León Mariscal, Beatriz, 49
Boff, Leonardo, 32
Bonaventure, 82
Brading, D. A. 91n4, 99n28
Burkhart, Louise M., 21, 23–24, 26–29, 33, 35, 52n62, 131
Bustamante, Francisco de, 34–35
Cabrera y Quintero, Cayetano de, 92, 98
Candlemas, 25
Castro, Antonio, 45, 58n88
Castilian, 72–73, 83
Catechesis, 20–24, 27, 34, 69–74, 81–82
Charles V, 72
Cihuacoatl, 11n24, 12n27
Coatlicue, 12, 12n27,
Communion, 73n27, 81
Confession, 75n27, 80
Correa, Juan, de 44–45, 53–57, 59, 60
Covenant 108–24
Cuadriello, Jaime, 42, 51–52, 54, 57
Daniel, Book of, 141, 144
Doak, Mary, 131, 145, 148–49
Echave Orio, Baltasar de, 43–46, 50, 59

Elizondo, Virgilio, ix, 76n32, 110, 118, 120, 125–33, 142–46
European traditions and Eurocentrism, 20–21, 26, 29, 33, 36–37, 47, 52, 80, 84–85, 109–11
Ezekiel, book of, 137, 140
Feasts, vii, viii, 4, 10, 14–18, 21, 24–26, 45, 136n51
Florencia, Francisco de, viii, 41
Florentine Codex, 1, 1n2,
Flor y canto, 128–29
Gante, Fray Pedro de, 28, 31–32, 66
Girard, René, viii, ix, 88–92, 102–7, 126–27, 147–49
Goizueta, Roberto, 118n30, 128n14, 139
Granziera, Patrizia, 13, 22
Historia general de las cosas de Nueva España (*General History of the Things of New Spain*), vii, 1–18, 35
Huitzilopochtli, 12, 12n27, 131n33, 150
Huei tlamahuiçoltica, viii, 36, 41, 42n6, 44, 57, 65–86, 134
Idolatry, 5, 7, 9, 10–12, 14–16, 81
Inculturation, viii, 26, 31, 34, 37, 85–86
Ita y Parra, Bartolomé Felipe de, viii, 93–107
Juan Bernardino, 55–56, 73n27, 77–80, 83, 122, 140
Juan Diego, 2, 34–36, 43n12, 45–46, 49–50, 53–60, 74–80, 108–10, 115–25, 129–30, 136–44, 150
  Apparition accounts/interpretations, ix, 1, 36, 40–46, 49–50, 53–60, 74–78, 81–83, 99, 108–12, 115–28, 130, 134, 136, 139n71, 140, 142–46, 148
  As prophet, 110–11, 125, 136–45
  In art, 42, 49, 53–60

155

index

Life and role as messenger, 74, 74n27, 76–80, 76n32, 83–85, 115–23, 129, 136–42
Tilma of, 2, 43n12, 42–46, 49, 53, 55, 60, 74–78, 83, 96, 96,121
Juárez, José, 46, 51, 56–57, 59
Kroger, Joseph, 13, 22
Lafaye, Jacques, 134, 144n97
Lara, Jaime, 68, 85
Latino theology, 128n11, 128n14, 146
León-Portilla, Miguel, 3n5, 4, 6n13, 131n32
Marian devotion, viii, 2, 15, 19–38, 77, 80, 85, 94
Matlazahuatl, viii, 90–92, 97–99, 103, 105–8
Matovina, Timothy, xi, 36, 48, 80, 109, 119, 134–36
Metz, Johann Baptist, ix, 126, 132n35, 147–50
Mexican eagle, 54, 54n69
Miracles, 14–17, 34–36, 46–53, 52n62, 56, 59, 74–79, 82–85, 89, 98, 133n43
Missionaries to New Spain, 2–15, 20–38, 65–73, 66n3, 80, 84–86, 150
Mosaic covenant, 112–16, 119–23
Mountains, 9, 13–17, 142n85
Nahuatl (language), ix, 1, 5–6, 10, 19–22, 24–25, 28, 31, 32–35, 37, 52n62, 57, 65, 71–75, 80–85, 128n10
Nahua religion, 3–14, 130–31, 133
  Gods, vii, 4–15, 11n24, 23, 89,
  Mingling with Christian traditions, 2, 10–13, 20, 67–68, 85–86, 109, 118
  Evangelization, vii–ix, 3–8, 11, 13, 15, 23, 53, 65–69, 81–85, 108–9, 129
Nican mopohua, ix, 20–21, 35–37, 53n68, 57n85, 74–76, 76n32, 83, 86, 99, 108–28, 134–39
Nican motecpana, 50, 74–79
Nican tlantica, 74
Niehta, Catharina de, 49, 62
Noahic covenant, 108, 112–17, 119, 122–23
Our Lady of Guadalupe
  Apparitions/interpretations, 34–35, 40, 50, 54–60, 75, 81–83, 99, 108–9, 115–20, 126–28, 130, 133n43, 134, 136, 139n71, 139–40, 142, 145–46, 148
  Art and Images, 39–62
  Edict of, 1637 39–40, 58
  Origins and rise, vii, viii
  In *Historia general de las cosas de Nueva España,* 2, 9–10
Our Lady of Guadalupe in Extremadura, 25, 52, 136, 136n51, 143, 144n98
Our Lady of Los Remedios, 58n88, 91, 94, 100–2, 106
Pardo, Osvaldo, 66n3
Pater Noster, 26, 28, 36, 70
Pentecost, 82
Peterson, Jeanette, 42–43, 43n13, 46, 46n31, 48–51, 56–58
Philip II, 73
Plague, 88–107
Poole, Stafford, 50
Pope Benedict XIV, vii, viii
Pope John Paul II, 108, 109n1
Prophets, 136–42
Quodvultdeus, 135
Revelation, 12, 44, 53–57, 126, 133, 135–36, 135n50
Rites and sacraments, 27, 69–75
Ruth and Naomi, 101
Sahagún, Bernardino de, vii–ix, 1–18, 20, 26, 31–32, 35
  Education, 3–4, 3n5
  "First anthropologist/ethnographer," 2, 4
  Historia general de las cosas de Nueva España, vii, ix, 1–8, 35
  Life purpose, 2, 4
  Psalmodia Christiana, 20–21, 31–32, 35
  View of Nahua practices, 2, 7–15
Salve Regina, 19, 26, 28–29, 36
Sánchez, Miguel, viii, ix, 40–44, 41n6, 46, 49n48, 50–59, 99, 111, 126–27, 134–36, 134n44, 138, 142–44, 146, 149
Sánchez Salmerón, Juan 44, 44n20

index

Sanneh, Lamin, 85
Siller Acuña, Clodomiro, 128n10
Spanish conquest, ix, 20, 23, 27, 109, 111, 118–19, 129–31, 136, 149–50
Stradanus, Samuel, vi, 46–52, 56, 59, 61–62
Teilhard de Chardin, Pierre 127, 127n8
Tepeyac (or Tepeyacac), 1–2, 9, 14–15, 21, 34–38, 44, 47–49, 54–56, 74–81, 92, 97–98, 102, 105, 121, 139, 142–43
Tonantzin, vii, 9–17, 35
Translation, 1, 3n7, 19–38
Trexler, Richard, 27

Toci, 10–17
University of Salamanca, 3
Vargas Lugo, Elisa, 42, 54n69, 58–59
Vega, Luis Laso de la viii, 20–21, 36–37, 40–42, 41n6, 44, 50–54, 53n68, 56–57, 59, 65, 73–86, 99, 128, 134
Veronica, 43, 43n12
Wills, 33
Woman clothed with the sun, 137
Zarza (burning bush), 94–97, 100, 103
Zumárraga, Bishop Juan de, 44, 51, 53n68, 55–56, 76–79, 110, 119–23, 125, 139–40

www.ingramcontent.com/pod-product-compliance
Lightning Source LLC
Chambersburg PA
CBHW050820160426
43192CB00010B/1840